AFRICAN VIOLETS

The Complete Guide

Joan Hill & Gwen Goodship

The Crowood Press

First published in 1995 by
The Crowood Press Ltd
Ramsbury, Marlborough
Wiltshire SN8 2HR

Paperback edition 1998

This impression 1999

British Library Cataloguing-in-Publication Data
A catalogue record for this book is available from the British
Library.

ISBN 1 86126 150 0

Dedication
For
Our friend, the late Ernest Fisher of Canada,
who gave us so much help and encouragement in
our early years of growing African violets.

Picture Credits
Colour photographs by Christopher Christodoulou,
Linda Neumann, William To, Nolan Blansit
Line-drawings by Claire Upsdale-Jones

Typeset by Dorwyn Ltd,
Rowlands Castle, Hants
Printed and bound by The Bath Press

CONTENTS

ACKNOWLEDGEMENTS

Grateful thanks are due to Christopher Christodoulou, Linda Neumann, William To and Nolan Blansit for photography. Our thanks also to John Manners of Green Gardener for helpful information on biological control of pests, and to Dr Charles L. Cole, Extension Entomologist of the Texas A & M University System for information on chemical control of pests on African violets.

INTRODUCTION

Who would have thought that the small, fleshy-leaved, deep blue-flowered plants found in East Africa a little over one hundred years ago would have been the harbinger of what today has become one of the world's most popular houseplants?

The *Saintpaulia*, or African violet as it is more commonly known, has progressed rapidly during the past fifty years from a few hundred different varieties to many thousands today in a wide range of colours and types. This is entirely due to the painstaking work of enthusiastic hybridists, mainly in the United States of America. For this reason the African Violet Society of America (AVSA), with its world-wide membership, has been recognized as the international registration body for the African violet. This society publishes annually a list of new hybrids, many of which are registered with it. These latter have been proved to the society to be stable by their hybridizers in colour and type of flower and foliage through several generations of vegetative propagation. Also, although a great percentage of new hybrids may not be registered with AVSA, they are known to be stable in form; it is just that the breeders have not applied for registration at the time of release to the public. Quite often many of these hybrids will be registered at a later date.

Hybridizing work continues today towards the time in the future when plants will have been bred having buttercup yellow flowers instead of the very pale primrose yellow of today. This would open the path to a range of flower colours which would include orange and true scarlet red, a possibility undreamed of some years ago, although there are hybridists who have been trying to produce yellow colouring in African violet flowers by intergeneric crossing for twenty years or more.

There are some who would like our African violets to have a perfume of some kind, although the species have none. In these days of genetic engineering anything seems possible. Personally, we prefer our African violets to remain without scent, but who is to say that we are right and others are wrong? It would be interesting to know what kind of perfume would be envisaged.

It must be understood that the African violet, a member of the *Gesneriaceae* family, bears no relationship to the garden violet of the *Violaceae* family. However, this is an often-voiced misconception. It has been known for African violets to have been planted in outdoor gardens in the

United Kingdom with this idea in mind, and the owner has been greatly disappointed when the plants died in the autumn.

Another error frequently made is to call *Saintpaulias* South African violets. This is patently wrong, because their habitat is entirely within a comparatively small area of East Africa and certainly not many thousands of miles to the south. It can also be said that the practice of prefixing a modern hybrid with *Saintpaulia ionantha* is wrong, since even very early hybridizing programmes for African violets were likely to have been carried out by crossing several of the other species with *S. ionantha* or *S. confusa*. Certainly today, the species themselves are rarely used in breeding, although some of their traits are still apparent in the new hybrids being produced today, such as the trailing type of miniature size.

It is our intention in this book to provide information on the African violet that will dissolve the myth that it is a difficult plant to grow successfully. There can be different ways of growing African violets, and whether the reader grows a hundred or more plants or just two or three on a window-sill, it is hoped that they may find within the following pages something of interest and help which will enable them to grow even better plants in their home.

1
HISTORY

THE FIRST SPECIES

Towards the end of the nineteenth century, East Africa was ruled by Germany through district officers, one of whom deserves the gratitude of houseplant enthusiasts today: this was Baron Walter von Saint Paul-Illaire who had an interest in botany. His father, Baron Ulrich von Saint Paul-Illaire, was a patron of the botanic garden at Herrinhausen near Hanover where Herman Wendland was director, and so Baron Walter would send plant material home whenever he found anything that looked interesting.

Whilst on a tour of his territory in 1892 in the coastal area near Tanga, Baron Walter found a colony of low-growing, hairy- and fleshy-leaved plants with small single flowers of intense blue. He collected samples of the live plants and seed capsules. Later in this tour of the East Usambara Mountains, he collected material from another colony of these plants at around 3,000ft (900m). All the plant material was sent to his father in Germany, who grew plants from the seed and shared them with Wendland. The latter, a taxonomist, realized that these plants were of an unknown genus, and it was he who described it and named it: *Saintpaulia* in honour of the Saint Paul-Illaires, and the species name *S. ionantha* from the Greek for a violet-like flower.

Although we know today that Baron Walter collected two species on his tour in 1892, it is apparent that Wendland had only considered the plant material collected at Tanga. The second sample of plant material collected in the East Usambara Mountains lived in botanic gardens as *S. kewensis*, a variant of *S. ionantha* until B.L. Burtt studied and identified it as a definite species in 1956 and named it *S. confusa*.

OTHER SPECIES

Over the years, more *Saintpaulia* species have been found by a number of collectors, some within two or three years of the first, and have been identified and described by B.L. Burtt and others. All the species have been found in a comparatively small region of East Africa and nowhere else in the world. At present the following are known: twenty identified

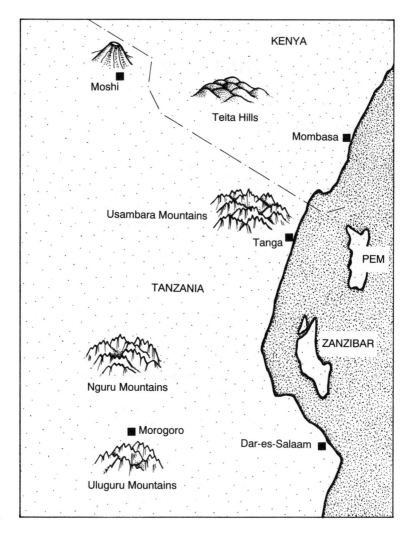

Areas of East Africa where Saintpaulia *species have been found.*

and described species, one other recently discovered, six variants and two natural hybrids; each has its own tiny separate habitat area.

All species have single flowers with five lobes, of which the upper two are smaller than the lower three, combining into a very short corolla attached to a calyx that has five sharp-pointed sepals. The flower colour is blue, ranging from a very pale shade that is nearly white, to deep purple. The leaves are variously hairy, the hairs ranging from few to many and

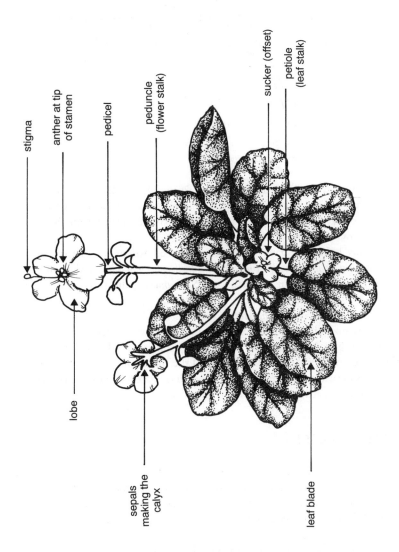

stigma

anther at tip of stamen

pedicel

peduncle (flower stalk)

sucker (offset)

petiole (leaf stalk)

lobe

sepals making the calyx

leaf blade

An African violet plant and its parts.

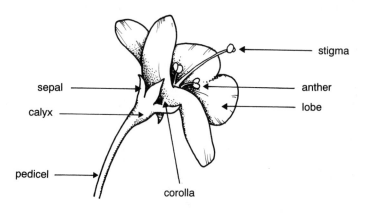

An African violet flower and its parts.

from short to long, in shades of green from light to dark. Some species are rosette-forming, with very short leaf internodes, whilst others have long internodes with trailing and branching growth. Also within the species the growth may be of large or tiny size.

Thus hybridists have been able to breed rosette types from species including *S. ionantha*, *S. confusa*, *S. difficilis*, *S. grandifolia* and *S. orbicularis*; miniature types from *S. pusilla* and *S. shumensis*, the former of which is now unfortunately extinct; and trailing types from *S. grotei*, *S. magungensis*, *S. m. minima* and *S. pendula*.

It is possible that there are still unidentified species somewhere out there in East Africa, and perhaps one day someone will add to the known number. Sadly many of the habitats of the species have been destroyed by land utilization, and the only sources of live material of many species now are botanic gardens and private collections.

THE SPECIES

S. brevipilosa   The two to six flowers of light purple with a darker eye per peduncle are short lived and hide amongst the thin, round light green leaves. It is a small-growing, single-crowned rosette plant. The flowers are 1in (2.5cm) in diameter and the leaves are 1.5in (4cm) across the blade.

S. confusa   The one or two flowers of dark purple per peduncle nestle on the darkish green, ovate leaves that have a very pale back. It can become a large multi-crowned rosette plant. The flowers are 1.25in (3cm) in diameter, and leaf blades grow up to 3in (8cm) long.

S. difficilis   The three to six flowers of medium blue per peduncle appear between the long petioled longifolia, yellowish-green leaves forming an upright rosette plant that is usually single crowned but may sucker. The flowers are only 0.75in (2cm) across, and the leaf blades are 2 to 3in (5 to 7.5cm) long and 2in (5cm) wide.

S. diplotricha   The two to four pale lilac flowers per peduncle grow above the purplish-green leaves which have slightly recurved margins, and as the specific name implies, hairs of two lengths. The flowers are about 1in (2.5cm) in diameter, and the lower lobes jut forwards. The leaves are of a similar size to *S. confusa* but slightly thicker. The plant grows as a flat single-crowned rosette.

S. goetzeana   This has two to three flowers of bicolour pale lilac per peduncle; these are infrequently found amid the nearly white, very hairy, light green leaves borne on short, hairy, branching and creeping stems. The flowers are 0.6in (1.5cm) in diameter, and the leaves are 1.25in (3cm) across the blade. This is a rather difficult plant to grow but worth while, nevertheless.

S. grandifolia   Up to twenty bright purple flowers per long peduncle appear between the long petioled, bright green, sometimes crinkled, very thin and almost translucent leaves which have blades 4in (10cm) in diameter. The small size of the 0.5in (1.3cm) diameter flowers is also amply compensated for by the numerous peduncles produced by this large-growing, single-crowned plant.

S. grotei   The two to four bicoloured violet flowers per very long peduncle appear between the leaf blades which have very long petioles, are coarsely toothed, and 4in (10cm) long. The 1.25in (3cm) diameter flowers are infrequent on this truly vining species, which can grow stems over 3ft (1m) long.

S. inconspicua   The one to six flowers are almost white with a blue centre eye, and the leaves are 2in (5cm) long and glabrous; together they make an untidy-looking, frail creeping plant which is now believed to be extinct in the wild. The flowers are tiny, barely 0.5in (1.3cm) in diameter.

S. intermedia   The five to seven blue flowers per peduncle are infrequently produced amid the 1in (2.5cm) round and serrated dark green leaves; these are hairy and tend to spoon. The plant is nearer to rosette growth than trailing.

S. ionantha   The two to eight variable violet flowers per peduncle grow above the leaves, which are nearly round, slightly serrated, and fleshy; they are dark green above and purplish below and have a tendency to spoon. The flowers are 1.25in (3cm) in diameter, and the leaf blades are up to 3in (8cm) long on this truly rosette-growing plant.

S. ionantha alba   This is a white-flowered variant of *S. ionantha*. It has a very similar description, although it is slightly smaller and not quite so sturdy in growth. It was found and identified in the late 1980s.

S. magungensis   The two to four dark blue flowers per peduncle virtually cover the nearly round, cupped-down, medium green leaves; these grow from a branching, procumbent stem which is 6in (15cm) long. The flowers are small, being 0.75in (2cm) across the lobes; the leaf blades are 2.75in (7cm) long. It is a trailing species and has been used in hybridizing.

S. m. var. *minima*   A small-growing variant that has one to two tiny flowers per peduncle, and thin, serrated, cupped-down leaves about half the size of *S. magungensis*.

S. m. var. *occidentalis*   Although a variant, it is similar to the species; it has two to five flowers per peduncle, and its leaves are thicker, more brittle and have a reddish coloration. The stems root down when in contact with compost.

S. nitida   The one to three deep violet flowers per peduncle are over-shadowed by the very glossy dark green leaves; these have 2in (5cm) long leaf blades which are nearly round. The flowers are 0.75in (2cm) across, and the plant grows as a small multi-crown.

S. orbicularis   The eight to ten flowers per peduncle can vary in colour from nearly white to light lilac blue with a violet centre eye, and are 1in (2.5cm) across. The thin, glossy leaf blades are nearly round, 2.75in (7cm) long, and light green in colour. The plant is truly rosette-growing.

S. o. var. *purpurea*   A variant of the species with darker coloured flowers, and round to heart-shaped dark green leaves.

S. pendula   One to two lavender flowers per peduncle grow from the many leaf axils, and make a floriferous plant due to the greatly branching stems. The nearly round, serrated leaves are 1.75in (4.5cm) long, and are thick, very hairy and yellow-green in colour. The flowers are 1in (2.5cm) across.

S. p. var. *kizarae*   A variant with darker coloured leaves on stalks tinged brownish-red; the flowers appear to be similar in size to the species. The plant can have more compact growth.

S. pusilla   There are one to three flowers per peduncle, with the top two lobes of mauve and the lower three of almost white. The flowers are barely 0.4in (1cm) across, and the tiny leaf blades are pointed, ovate, and coloured green with a purple back; they are 1.25in (3cm) long. The unbranched stem makes it the tiniest of all the species. Sadly, it is thought to be extinct even in private collections now.

S. rupicola   There are up to six medium blue flowers per peduncle which grow from the axils of largish leaves of medium green; these are long petioled and slightly hairy. The flowers are 1in (2.5cm) in diameter, and the leaf blade measures 3in (7.5cm) long and 2in (5cm) wide. The plant stem tends to grow sideways, and it is multi-crowned.

S. shumensis   There are up to five flowers per peduncle, pale mauve with a violet splash at the base of the two upper lobes; they are 0.75in (2cm) across. The small leaves are nearly round with toothed margins and a pebbly surface; they are 1.25in (3cm) long, pale to dark green in colour, and are reddish along the veins on the back. A small-growing rosette plant, although it may sucker to some extent.

S. teitensis   There is only one light blue flower per peduncle on this species, each one being 1in (2.5cm) across; they hide beneath the glossy leaves of dark green above and reddish-purple below. The leaf blades are 3in (7.5cm) long and 2in (5cm) wide.

S. tongwensis   The four to six lavender flowers per peduncle and the hairy, elliptic leaves together make a floriferous plant. The flowers are 1.25in (3cm) across, the leaves 3.5in (9cm) long and 2in (5cm) wide. This is a rosette-forming plant which grows as an upright single crown; it is comparatively easy to grow.

S. velutina   With up to six small flowers per peduncle and many peduncles, this is a very floriferous species. The medium violet flowers have a darker centre eye, and some lobes are tipped with white. The flowers are 0.75in (2cm) in diameter. The nearly round, serrated and velvety leaves are very dark green on the upper surface, with a reddish-purple back; they are 1.5in (4cm) long. This is also a species which is comparatively easy to grow.

S. Robertson   As yet not officially described, it has medium to deep violet-blue flowers standing upright on strong stems. The medium green leaves are slightly serrated and elongated with a velvet texture. It is large-growing.

S. 'House of Amani'   This is probably a natural hybrid rather than a species, but should be listed. It has five to seven lavender blue flowers per peduncle which are short-lived and grow above the pointed and quilted dark green leaves; these have a red lower surface and petiole. It usually grows as a single-crowned rosette.

S. 'Sigi Falls'   This too, is probably a natural hybrid. It has flowers of variable violet, and thick ovate leaves of dark green with prominent, very pale veins on the upper surface whilst the lower surface is red in colour. Both flowers and leaves are variable in size.

S. amaniensis   This has now been recognized as a variant of *S. magungensis*, and so has been deleted as a separate species. It has two or three flowers of blue violet with a darker eye, about 1in (2.5cm) across per peduncle. The leaves are ovate, glossy, and medium green, about 1.5in (4cm) long and 1in (2.5cm) wide. The branching stems are about 4in (10cm) long.

HYBRIDIZING IN THE USA

About thirty-five years after the discovery of the *Saintpaulia*, the American nursery of Armacost and Royston in Los Angeles recognized the possibilities of this plant being successfully grown in the home, and decided to import seed and leaves from Suttons in England and Ernst Benary in Germany. They produced from these imports an initial selection of one thousand plants; later, a further selection reduced that number to one hundred plants. During the next five years these were flowered and propagated by leaf to find the best varieties. After this period of time, only ten were considered good enough to be marketed to the public, in the mid-1930s. These ten varieties are now known as the 'Original Ten', of which eight were from the English import and two from the German. All flowers are in the blue to purple range and are single. They are still grown today, and are named 'Admiral', 'Amethyst', 'Blue Boy', 'Commodore', 'Mermaid', 'Neptune', 'Norseman', 'No. 32', 'Sailor Boy' and 'Viking'.

Of these it was 'Blue Boy' that became the most important ancestor of the vast number of hybrids available today: it was the only one to mutate naturally and hold the recessive red gene. Firstly, in 1939 it produced a plant with double blue flowers. Secondly, a year later it produced a plant with single pink flowers which was named 'Pink Beauty'; and then in 1941 'Blue Boy' naturally mutated again to give a plant that was named 'Blue Girl'. This variety had leaves with a white-coloured area stretching into the leaf blade from the petiole; hence the term 'girl' leaf to differentiate it from the plain 'boy' type leaf of 'Blue Boy'. These terms have given rise to the idea that there are 'boy' and 'girl' plants needed for hybridization. However, this is not the case, as all African violets are bisexual whether or not they have 'boy' or 'girl' leaves.

The first pure white flower, 'White Lady', came in 1942 from a cross between pink and blue flowered plants. In the following years, further hybridizing produced plants with flowers having a thin white edge to the lobes, given the type name 'geneva' (having been bred at the Geneva Nursery); and then star-shaped flowers with five lobes of equal size. The first double pink hybrid came from the Lyndon Lyon nurseries in 1954.

The next important development in African violets was natural mutation to variegated foliage. In 1957 a leaf from the green-leaved 'White Pride' produced a plantlet having a narrow white edge on its leaves, and this gave rise to the variegate 'Tommie Lou'. It was named for Mrs Tommie Lou Oden who, before releasing her variety to the public, proved its stability through nine generations of vegetative propagation of leaf.

Also in the late 1950s, Ethel Champion produced a second type of variegate in which the very young centre leaves were white but turned green on maturity. This type is now called crown or Champion variegation. Then in 1961 the green-leaved hybrid 'Lilian Jarrett' gave a plantlet that was seen to have leaves speckled with white in a mosaic pattern: hence mosaic or Jarrett variegation, though the original 'Lilian Jarrett' green-leaved hybrid is never seen nowadays. These three variegated foliage plants were the forebears of all the variegated hybrids available today.

So keen were the hybridists to increase the numbers of varieties that some turned from hybridizing to using chemicals such as colchicine and giberellic acid to treat African violet material to encourage mutations. Others irradiated material to produce mutants. Exactly which varieties were produced by these means we do not know, but certainly the 1960s and 1970s saw the beginning of an explosion in the numbers of new African violets, and this was not just the result of crossing two plants to obtain seed.

In the 1960s the semi-miniature and miniature-sized African violets had been established by hybridization between the miniature species *S. pusilla* and *S. shumensis* and selected small-growing varieties of previous hybrids. At the same time, breeding programmes using *S. grotei* had founded the trailing hybrids, and during the 1970s the miniature, semi-miniature and trailing types were being marketed by nurseries.

EUROPEAN HYBRIDS

Whilst all the changes in African violets were happening in the United States, in Europe we looked to the German hybridists to breed plants to be marketed to the general public through florist shops. Such plants had to be strong enough to withstand the rigours of being transported by road from the good conditions prevailing in the nurseries where they were propagated, to the adverse conditions in wholesale markets where they were sold, and thence to florist shops where they might be crushed amongst other plants and cut flowers, and chilled. They had to have long-lasting flowers on stiff stalks held well above the leaves, and to be able to survive being kept in homes that were not at that time centrally heated.

The 'Diana' series of 'Englert' had these virtues, with the exception of long-lasting flowers. Like all single-flowered hybrids at this time, the 'Dianas' dropped their blooms as soon as they became fully open. Compared with today's hybrids, the colour range was very limited in that it comprised only blue, red, pink and white solid colours.

It was another German hybridist, Hermann Holtkamp, whose work was rewarded by the production of non-dropping single-flowered hybrids. As the flowers of double hybrids did not drop but remained on the plant until they faded and died, he bred just enough of the doubleness trait into the single-flowered hybrids to produce this non-dropping strain. This became the 'Rhapsodie' series of African violets in a wider range of shades, colours and types of flower including star type. Early 'Rhapsodies' may still be seen in florists and garden centres today, as well as more modern 'Rhapsodie' hybrids and their cousins the 'Optimara' hybrids, so proving their lasting popularity and quality.

A further development came with the 'Ballet' series of African violets, bred by Arnold Fischer of Hanover. These plants had ruffled and fringed edges to the lobes, together with all the good qualities of the 'Rhapsodies' and an even wider colour range. The series name 'Ballet' was given to them to compare their flowers with the frilled tutu worn by ballet dancers. The 'Ballets' also may still be found in florists and garden centres today.

LATER FLOWER TYPES

During the past twenty years other types of African violet flowers have been hybridized. There are now the multicolours, having flowers with two or more different main colours, and also the bicolours with flowers having two or more shades of the same colour. Following these there are the fantasy types which have their flowers splashed and speckled with a colour different to the major one. However, the fantasies do have a possible fault in that their colour pattern can be unstable, and then their flowers revert to one solid colour. All these are available in all the types of African violet mentioned earlier.

The next progression was to the chimera or pinwheel type of plant. This has lobes with a central lengthways stripe of one colour sandwiched by stripes of either another shade of that colour or of a different colour. This formation is caused by two genetically different colour tissues growing side by side, and the type was recognized by Hugh Eyerdom of Granger Gardens in Ohio as having to be propagated in a different manner to the normal leaf propagation for true reproduction of the colour pattern. It can only be guessed at the number of earlier pinwheels that were lost because they were considered to be completely unstable by leaf propagation.

The latest American breakthrough in African violets came in the early 1990s, when hybrids were produced with splashes or streaks of pale primrose yellow on white or pink flowers. These hybrids should lead ultimately to hybrids with solid deep buttercup-yellow flowers, and thence to flowers of orange and true scarlet red in the future.

WORLD-WIDE HYBRIDS

Nowadays African violets are bred and grown all round the world. Many early Canadian hybrids came from Ernest Fisher, and many are still to be found in collections today. He has been followed by Sandra Lex, Michel Tremblay, Denis Croteau and others who have given us many notable hybrids. In Australia the 'Colonial' series of African violets by Hams of Blackwood Violets in Adelaide have been named for places, towns and cities in Australia; they are popular there, and some grow well in the United Kingdom, even though they are so far from their homeland. A nursery in Japan has a large collection of hybrids that have mutated to chimera plants. Varieties have been bred in New Zealand and South Africa, some of which are being grown in collections in the United Kingdom, and we have also had news of hybrids in Russia.

In England there is the 'Chiffon' series hybridized by Joan Hill; these grow very well under the conditions we can give them either on window-sills or under fluorescent lighting. Several 'Chiffons' have been registered with the AVSA.

Thus today the African violet is truly a world-wide houseplant, which has come very far since the species were first found in that small region of East Africa over a century ago.

2

CLASSIFICATION

TYPES OF PLANT

There are three main types of African violet: rosette, trailing, and variegated.

Rosette
This type of plant has a short main stem with very short internodes; the leaf petioles or stalks grow in layered whorls from the centre growth point. Depending upon the nature of the plant size, the single crown rosette may be any diameter from 2in (5cm) to over 2ft (60cm). Leaf blade size determines the diameter across a single crown at maturity; however, as a general rule, a plant in perfect condition will have up to five layers of leaves. Usually from each leaf axil a flower peduncle or stalk will arise which may bear one to ten individual flowers, each one on a slender pedicel. The flowers open fully in succession until the peduncle has the appearance of a multi-headed inflorescence.

Trailing
These African violets are likely to have long main stems with some distance between internodes. Leaf petioles are usually long in comparison to rosette types, and again grow out in layered whorls making a plant with more open growth. Trailers cannot be grown as single-crowned plants because side stems grow from some leaf axils forming branches, whilst flower peduncles grow from others. This branching of the main stem leads to the trailing appearance, as none of these branches is sturdy enough for upright growth.

Early trailing hybrids bred from *S. grotei* did, literally, trail from their containers. However, later hybrids bred by crossing other trailing species, such as *S. magungensis*, with rosette-type hybrids do not grow such long stems, and although multi-branched, these are often termed 'semi-trailing' due to their shorter, more sideways growth.

It should be noted that trailing African violets do not trail to anywhere near the extent to which houseplants such as *Tradescantia* or *Hedera* will.

Variegated Foliage
There are three basic types of variegation in African violets to be seen on the upper surface of their leaves: 'Tommie Lou' with a white-edged leaf;

crown, where the young centre leaves are white turning green as they reach maturity; and mosaic, having leaves speckled with white. Over the years hybridists have interbred these types so that white-edged leaves may also show crown and/or mosaic traits. Further breeding programmes have resulted in the variegation becoming cream, yellow, tan, pink and red as well as white in colour on green. Rosette and trailing types of African violets can have variegated foliage.

SIZE OF PLANTS

Modern hybrids of African violets have a wide size range across a single crown when fully mature, so much so that classification of size has come into being over the years. It is important that plants are correctly sized, especially when taking part in competitive exhibition. There are four main size ranges, and these are termed *miniature, semi-miniature, standard* and *large*.

Miniature
This size of hybrid grows up to 6in (15cm) across a single crown of a mature plant. Flowers and leaves are small in comparison, the flowers being about 0.75in (2cm) in diameter, and the leaf blades about 1in (2.5cm) long when full grown. Now that there are very small hybrids being produced, the term *micro-miniature* can also be seen in catalogues, usually describing plants with a diameter of less than 3in (7.5cm) across a single crown. These hybrids can have flowers and leaves of even smaller size.

Semi-Miniature
For exhibition purposes these hybrids must be more than 6in (15cm) and less than 8in (20cm) in diameter across a single crown at maturity. Their flowers can be nearly the same size as a small-growing standard-sized plant with their leaves about three-quarters the size. The quantity of flower is comparable to their size.

Standard
This size of plant will grow to over 8in (20cm) in diameter across a single crown, but must not exceed 16in (40cm) at maturity. Confusion can occur with the term 'standard' where in other plants it describes a specimen which has a long, bare stem or trunk below a head of foliage and flowers – rather than the measurement across the crown of leaves of an African violet. Flowers can be up to 2in (5cm) across the lobes, and leaf blades up to 3in (7.5cm) long.

Large

Large hybrids are those which grow to more than 16in (40cm) across a single crown at maturity; it has been known for such a plant to reach a diameter of around 3ft (1m). The leaf blades can be as much as 6in (15cm) long, and 4 to 5in (10 to 12.5cm) wide, and individual flowers may be up to 3in (7.5cm) across their lobes. Obviously these are not plants to be grown to their full potential on a window-sill.

With trailing hybrids there could be some confusion with sizing due to their manner of growth. However, although the entire trailing plant can be rather large, the relevant hybrid size is still taken as the measurement across one single crown. Therefore trailing hybrids also fall within the four ranges of size listed.

TYPES OF FLOWER

Single

This type of flower is that of all the species. It has five rounded *lobes*, as opposed to petals, in that they are joined at their base to form a very short corolla, whereas petals are individually separated. The upper two lobes are smaller than the lower three. One pair of stamens is present in single flowers. Two recent terms should be described here: *stick-tight* refers to non-dropping single flowers, and *pansy* refers to the original single flower shape.

Semi-double

These flowers have a single layer of lobes and a small tuft or crest of tiny lobes around the stamens. The crest may be of lobes up to half the size of the outer lobes, and does not form a complete layer. Usually there are two or more pairs of stamens present indicating that they are not single flowers.

Double

Two or more complete layers of lobes, which are more often than not of the same size, are termed double flowers. However, the most frequently seen double flower will have a minimum of three layers and often more. Some are nowadays described as being a full double, a triple, or carnation-like. Once again, two or more pairs of stamens can be seen, and some of the stamens appear as tiny yellow swellings at the base of the lobe.

Star

A single star flower has five slightly pointed lobes all of the same size. In a double star flower, the outer layer has lobes of equal size whilst the inner layers may be of unequal size.

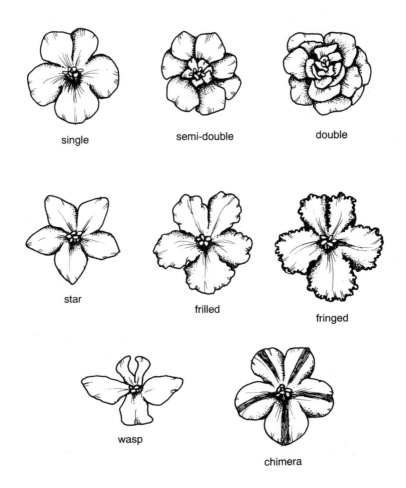

single   semi-double   double

star   frilled   fringed

wasp   chimera

Types of flower.

Bell

This is a flower that cannot open fully to a flat face because the lobes are joined to their outer edge more than they would be normally. It invariably appears to be single, although there may be six or seven lobes. The presence of two pairs of stamens shows that in fact the form is semi-double.

Wasp

This is a single flower where the top two lobes are much narrower and smaller than the lower three, thus giving the impression of the outline of a wasp or fly. This type of flower is not often seen nowadays, although it was fairly popular in hybrids some twenty years ago.

Tubular
This type of flower is rarely seen in present-day hybrids, and is purely a collector's item. A tube is formed by the margins of the lobes turning back behind the upper lobes.

Fluted
In this type, each lobe is ruffled lengthways, as in a fan. It may be single, semi-double or double in form.

Ruffled
Each lobe has a slightly undulating edge, and once again may be single, semi-double or double in form.

Frilled
Each lobe is more undulating than the ruffled type of flower, even to the extent that it could be said to be wavy.

Fringed
The edges of the lobes are so frilled as to give the impression of an Elizabethan ruff. The fringe is frequently of a colour different to that of the lobes, and the flower may be single, semi-double or double.

Geneva
This term is given to a flower which has a thin white edge to the lobes. It was derived from a plant raised on the Geneva Nursery in California, USA, in the late 1940s. Sometimes the white edge is so thin as to disappear, but it will return in later flowering.

Bordered
Flowers with a wide coloured band on their edge are termed *bordered*. The colour of the border may be a shade of the colour of the lobes, or an entirely different colour, or even white. If the latter, the border is much wider than in a geneva, which is why the flower may not be termed as such.

Bicolour
This term seems to have a different meaning in African violets than in other plants, because it denotes a flower with two or more shades of one colour as opposed to two different colours. Often in catalogues a *bicolour* may also be described as a *two-tone*.

Multicolour

These flowers have two or more different colours in their lobes. Flowers on each peduncle may also be inconsistent in their colour pattern in that some could be of one solid colour whilst others are multicoloured. This is probably a sign of instability.

Fantasy

In these flowers the main colour of the lobes is speckled and/or splashed with another colour. It may be single, semi-double or double in form, and is sometimes unstable in pattern.

Chimera

A flower of this type may be a bicolour or a multicolour in that the lobes are striped centrally along their length either with one shade of a colour or with a different colour to that of the sides of the lobe. Originally there were only single-flowered chimeras, now there are semi-double and double-flowered plants.

TYPES OF LEAF

Boy

The all-green leaf most commonly seen on African violets: it is very like the leaves of S. *ionantha* and S. *confusa*. The term derives from the early hybrid 'Blue Boy'. It is now more frequently described as 'plain' or 'tailored' and at times as 'show foliage', although very many African violets have something more than plain leaves.

Girl

In this type the leaf petiole extends into the leaf blade as a white or very pale green area at its base. The leaf blade is more fleshy than boy types and often has a scalloped edge and a slightly pointed tip. The term comes from 'Blue Girl' which was a mutation from 'Blue Boy'. There is no sexual connotation to the two terms.

Ovate

The leaf blade is oval in shape, the length being greater than the width. It is often combined with quilted leaves.

Pointed

The tip of the leaf blade is more pointed than in the boy type, and can indeed be sharply pointed. The leaf blade surface may be smooth and somewhat glossy.

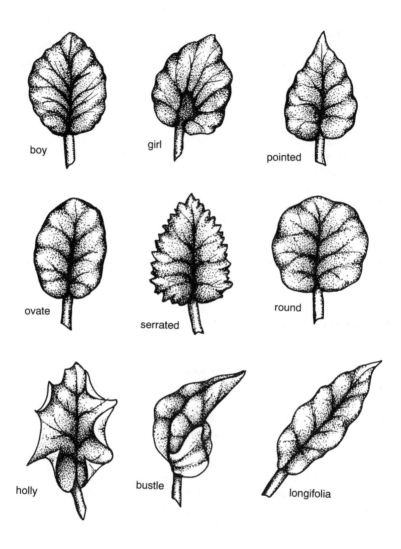

Types of leaf.

Round
The length and width of the leaf blade are equal in length. This type is frequently seen combined with girl leaves.

Heart–Shaped
The tip of the leaf blade is pointed, and at its base extends roundly on either side of the leaf petiole. Quite often the blade is smoothly flat.

Longifolia
The leaf blade is much longer in length than in width, the latter being comparatively narrow when compared with the ovate type. The upper surface of the blade can be quite hairy, and its tip is often pointed. This type has even been mistaken for a young *Streptocarpus* leaf.

Bustle
The base of the leaf blade on either side of the petiole extends backwards and curls up to form secondary leaves, giving the impression of a bustle on the back of the leaf. It was often seen in hybrids some years ago, but is rare nowadays.

Quilted
This term refers to the puckered, raised areas of the leaf blade lying between the veins as in quilting. It is probably the most frequently seen type of present-day hybrid.

Strawberry
The leaf blade is puckered, and its hairs grow from tiny raised points on the blade, as on the surface of a strawberry plant's leaf.

Ruffled
The edge of this type of leaf is very slightly undulating.

Wavy
This describes a leaf blade with an undulating edge; the term is used more frequently than 'ruffled' for a leaf.

Holly
The edge of this leaf blade is much more deeply undulating, making a shape very similar to a prickly holly tree leaf.

Scalloped
This leaf blade has a broadly rounded toothed edge, as in an embroidered scalloped edge.

Serrated
The edge of this leaf blade is sharply toothed, in the same way as material cut with a dressmaker's pinking shears; frequently the blade tip is also pointed.

Spooned
The entire leaf edge is upturned so that the blade forms a depression, as in a spoon. This leaf type may also be described as 'cupped-up'.

Colour

Other than in the variegated hybrids, the upper surface of African violet leaves comes in all shades of green from very pale through to very dark, almost black, green. Similarly, the colour of the lower surface may range from almost white through to pale green, to pink, to very dark red. The red pigmentation is due to the presence of anthrocyanins in the leaves which may be natural in the hybrid or can be produced during adverse growing conditions.

Variegates　Variegated foliage appears in all the previously described types of leaf. It can be of white on green, or cream, yellow, tan, pink or red in any combination on green, and is seen solely on the upper surface of the leaves. It is so attractive in a well grown African violet that in periods of rest from flower production the plant may look just as beautiful. In these cases flowering becomes an added bonus.

Very often several of these leaf types will appear in the foliage of a plant, such as in an ovate, scalloped, wavy variegated leaf or a serrated, spooned, pink-backed leaf.

As all the types of flower and leaf described here can be seen on all the sizes of rosette, trailing and variegated plants, it can be seen how wide is the variety of African violets available. In fact there are so many thousands of different hybrids grown around the world that it is certainly impossible to have every one of them in a collection.

3

AFRICAN VIOLET HYBRIDS

We have had great difficulty in selecting the following hybrids from the many hundreds that we have grown during the past twenty-five years or more, and from those that we are growing now. They should all grow well in home conditions and give great enjoyment to their growers. Those hybrids that have been registered with the African Violet Society of America (AVSA) have their registration number at the end of their description. The larger this number is, the newer the registration, although it is possible that the hybrid was on the market for two, three or even more years prior to registration.

It should be understood that it is very difficult to identify from the following official descriptions an African violet bought un-named from a garden centre or florist. Growing conditions do alter the appearance of African violets as to colouring, and in any event, always remember that colours are in the eye of the beholder. Also, in the present day, there are many African violets that could be termed look-a-likes, with only a subtle difference in appearance and so easily mistaken for one another. Therefore do not put a name from these descriptions to an un-named African violet, as that could cause even more confusion.

STANDARD OR LARGE HYBRIDS

'ACA's Vasco'
Semi-double, pink star with a red eye and purple fantasy spots. Tailored, dark green variegated leaves. Small standard. Brownlie, Canada. This is a beautiful plant, but like many fantasies it may throw up a solid purple flower. If this happens, the flower should be removed.

'Alouette'
Double, fringed, pale pink with a lighter edge. Tailored, slightly wavy, hairy, scalloped variegate of green, cream and pink. Large. I. Fredette, USA. AVSA Reg. No. 2787. A glorious hybrid. However, it can be very difficult to propagate by leaf. The pink of the flowers and variegation match in colour. We have included 'Alouette' because of its great beauty.

'Ballet Lisa'
Single to semi-double, fringed, pink. Tailored, medium green leaves. Standard. A. Fischer, Germany. AVSA Reg. No. 2898. One of the first 'Ballet' series released. An easy grower, which after so many years of propagation is now showing a little of its inbred doubleness.

'Ballet Marta'
Single to semi-double, fringed, violet bicolour. Tailored, medium green leaves. Standard. A. Fischer, Germany. AVSA Reg. No. 2899. Also one of the first 'Ballet' series and easy to grow.

'Barbara Jean'
Double, dark pink. Plain, medium green leaves. Large. E. Fisher, Canada. Still a good show plant despite its age.

'Belizaire'
Double star of two-tone purple with darker veins. Glossy, serrated dark green leaves variegated with pink and cream. Large. J. Domiano, USA. AVSA Reg. No. 7111. Very floriferous, and shapes into a symmetrical plant easily, making it a good show plant.

'Blue Boy'
Single, dark violet-blue. Plain, ovate, medium green leaves. Standard. Armacost and Royston. AVSA Reg. No. (41) AVS-48. One of the 'Original Ten'.

'Bright Eyes'
Single, dark blue flowers with prominent yellow pollen sacs. Tailored dark green leaves. Standard. African Violet Centre, England. A popular hybrid in the UK, and an easy-to-grow plant.

'Centenary'
Semi-double to double, royal purple with a white edge. Round, medium green leaves. Standard. African Violet Centre, England. Named for the centenary of the discovery of the African violet, this hybrid is floriferous and grows well.

'Chiffon Charm'
Double, lavender. Plain, medium green leaves. Standard. J. Hill, England. AVSA Reg. No. 5968. As the expression goes: it blooms like crazy!

'Chiffon Cream'
Semi-double to double, fluted, creamy-white. Round, serrated, quilted,

very dark green leaves with a red back. Standard. J. Hill, England. The flowers of this hybrid are at least 2in (5cm) in diameter, and the plant is a symmetrical grower.

'Chiffon Harmony'
Double, fluted, pale pink. Tailored, light green leaves. Standard. J. Hill, England. A very early and prolific bloomer.

'Chiffon Maritime Variegated'
Semi-double, frilled, bright blue with a darker eye and a thin white geneva edge. Plain, quilted, medium green leaves that are crown variegated with cream and pink. Standard. J. Hill, England, AVSA Reg. No. 7932. A foliage mutation of 'Chiffon Maritime' that grows single crown without help.

'Chiffon Masquerade'
Semi-double lilac. Tailored, dark green leaves variegated with cream and pink. Standard. J. Hill, England. AVSA Reg. No. 6928. A good show plant because the foliage shapes easily and well, with many upright flower stalks.

'Chiffon Moonmoth'
Single to semi-double, dark blue. Tailored, dark green leaves. Standard. J. Hill, England. AVSA Reg. No. 7933. A compact-growing plant that makes a good show plant.

'Chiffon Pageant'
Single to semi-double, medium pink. Quilted, dark green leaves variegated with cream and pink. Standard. J. Hill, England, AVSA Reg. No. 6929. A show stopper which has won many prizes over the years.

'Chiffon Quilt'
Single, slightly frilled, royal blue with a darker eye. Heavily quilted, dark green leaves with a red back. Standard. J. Hill, England. One of the latest hybrids in the 'Chiffon' series. It has a stunning flower colour and grows symmetrically.

'Chiffon Sparkle'
Single to semi-double, star of deep lavender. Heart-shaped dark green leaves with a red back. Large. J. Hill, England. The many flower stalks stand up well above the foliage in a bouquet. Given good growing conditions this hybrid may grow to nearly 20in (50cm) in diameter.

'Chiffon Vesper'
Single to semi-double, star of lilac. Tailored, glistening, velvety dark green leaves. Large standard. J. Hill, England. The distinctive foliage grows into a flat and symmetrical rosette with many large flowers.

'Colonial Canberra'
Single to semi-double, frilled, cerise pink and white with a darker eye. Tailored, light green leaves. Standard. Hams, Blackwood Violets, Adelaide, Australia. A small-sized standard violet that makes a good window-sill plant.

'Colonial Hahndorf'
Single to semi-double, frilled star of bicolour mauve. Tailored, medium green leaves. Standard. Hams, Blackwood Violets, Adelaide, Australia. A large-growing standard with flowers 2.5 to 3in (6.5 to 7.5cm) in diameter. A good show plant.

'Colonial Kosciusko'
Semi-double white that may have a blush of very pale pink. Tailored, light green leaves. Standard. Hams, Blackwood Violets, Adelaide, Australia. A very worthwhile hybrid to grow and makes a good show plant.

'Colonial Mildura'
Semi-double dark maroon. Tailored, dark green leaves. Standard. Hams, Blackwood Violets, Adelaide, Australia. This hybrid from Australia grows well under UK conditions. The flower colour is very striking.

'Colonial Roseworthy'
Double, rose pink. Plain, medium green leaves. Standard. Hams, Blackwood Violets, Adelaide, Australia. A very floriferous hybrid with flowers almost hiding the foliage.

'Crystallaire'
Double star of medium blue with a strong white edge. Plain, pointed light green leaves. Large. Eyerdom, Granger Gardens, USA. AVSA Reg. No. 4295. A popular hybrid. The white edge emphasizes the colour and shape of the flower.

'Delft'
Semi-double, cornflower blue. Tailored, medium green leaves. Standard. J. Hill, England. Makes a very good show plant with many large flowers. It has been said to rival 'Granger's Wonderland'.

'Delft Imperial'
Double, fringed, geneva, blue bicolour. Pointed, quilted, scalloped dark green leaves. Standard. Eyerdom, Granger Gardens, USA. AVSA Reg. No. 1326. A very old favourite. Easy to grow and shapes well for show purposes.

'Dumplin''
Double, two-tone pink. Plain, quilted, medium green leaves. Large. AVSA Reg. No. 3931. A hybrid with many very large flowers. An easy-to-grow plant.

'Emi'
Semi-double to double, light blue with a geneva edge. Pointed, serrated medium green leaves. Standard. Although of unknown origin this hybrid is frequently to be seen in florists and garden centres. It is likely not to be labelled, but it is a distinctive hybrid.

'Emma Louise'
Double, coral pink. Tailored, dark green, red-backed leaves. Standard. M. Garford, African Violet Centre, England. Striking-coloured flowers on a plant that grows well.

'Fancy Pants'
Single, frilled white with a fuchsia border. Tailored, medium green leaves. Standard. Hybrid from USA. Unfortunately the fuchsia colouring is nowadays very variable, but the plant is still worth growing.

'Fantaisie Florale'
Semi-double to double star of pink with medium blue speckled fantasy. Quilted, serrated, medium green leaves with a red back. Standard. Croteau, Canada. AVSA Reg. No. 7037. An impressive hybrid that stays fantasy type in flower. Worth growing as something different to the norm.

'Favorite Child'
Semi-double, slightly frilled white, with medium blue centre and edge. Tailored, medium green, flat and symmetrically growing leaves. Standard. B. Johnson, USA. AVSA Reg. No. 7676. The late Bill Johnson thought this hybrid embodied all the attributes of violetry and that it was excellent for breeding. It is very floriferous and very worth growing. Please note that when grown in a collection it must be labelled with the American spelling.

'Fisherman's Paradise'
Double, deep lavender with a fringed purple edge. Pointed, medium green leaves variegated with white. Large. B. Sisk, USA. AVSA Reg.

No. 4843. An oldish hybrid that has stood the test of time and is still winning prizes.

'Fleur de Mai'
Single, geneva star of dusky coral. Plain, very dark green, nearly black, leaves. Standard. Tremblay, Canada. A spectacular colour combination of leaf and flower. Well worth growing, as are many of the breeding from this Canadian hybridist.

'Frosted Whisper'
Single, stick-tight star of white. Quilted, wavy, medium green leaves variegated with cream. Large. Scott, USA. AVSA Reg. No. 7198. Grown under good conditions, this plant has a mass of glistening white flowers that stand up well above the crisp foliage.

'Futaba'
Single to semi-double, medium to dark blue. Tailored, quilted, dark green leaves with a red back. Standard. From Holland. A good window-sill plant.

'Ghost Dance
Double, frilled star of white that may be touched with green. Slightly quilted, light to medium green leaves. Standard. K. Stork, USA. AVSA Reg. No. 7707. The many flowers stand well above the flat symmetrical foliage. It grows best under lower light intensities, as is often the case with white flowers.

'Granger's Wonderland'
Semi-double, frilled, light blue. Wavy, olive green leaves. Large. Eyerdom, Granger Gardens, USA. AVSA Reg. No. 3419. Although first marketed nearly thirty years ago, this hybrid is still winning prizes at major African violet competitive shows around the world. No need to say that it is well worth growing.

'Happy Cricket'
Double, frilled, two-tone lavender. Ruffled, dark green leaves with a red back. Large. Hollada, USA. AVSA Reg. No. 5726. An excellent blooming, older hybrid with large-sized flowers.

'Ice Maiden'
Single star of white with blue markings in the centre. Tailored, medium green leaves. Standard. African Violet Centre, England. An easy-to-grow hybrid for UK conditions.

'Jean-Pierre Croteau'
Semi–double star of dark purple, spotted and splashed with deep coral fantasy. Quilted and serrated dark green leaves. Large. D. Croteau, Canada. AVSA Reg. No. 7038. A symmetrically growing hybrid with unusual colouring.

'Judy Partain'
Semi–double, deep pink. Tailored, medium green leaves variegated with white. Large. B. Sisk, USA. AVSA Reg. No. 6769. This is a really large grower with leaves that are easily as large as your hand, as the saying goes. Not really one for the window-sill.

'Jupiter'
Single, light to medium blue, usually with a white edge. Modified girl leaf of dark green with a red back. Standard. Origin unknown, but certainly available in the UK. The modified girl leaf allows this hybrid to be symmetrical and flat-growing. Can make a good plant for show.

'Karinya Queen'
Full double, rich pink. Serrated, dark green leaves variegated with cream. Large standard. M. Taylor, Australia (from seed of R. Nadeau, USA). A large-flowered hybrid that grows and shapes easily and well. The flower colour stands out against the foliage colour.

'King's Treasure'
Double star of dark lavender banded in purple and with a slightly frilled white edge that is often marked with green. Ovate, serrated, medium green leaves. Large standard. Lyon/Sorano, USA. AVSA Reg. No. 7210. The unusual colouring of the many flowers makes this an outstanding hybrid. It is fairly easy to grow to a very good-looking show plant.

'Lady Diana'
Single to semi-double, lavender with a darker edge. Quilted, medium green leaves. Large. E. Fisher, Canada. AVSA Reg. No. 4441. If you like lavender-coloured flowers, this hybrid will please you. Named for Diana, Princess of Wales before her marriage.

'Leone'
Semi-double maroon with pink fantasy flecks. Tailored, medium green leaves. Large. E. Fisher, Canada. Another popular show plant that keeps its fantasy pattern.

'Lilian Jarrett'
Double, light pink with pointed lobes. Pointed, serrated, light green

leaves with mosaic variegation of white. Standard. Tinari, USA. AVSA Reg. No. 2902. Another very old favourite. Grows to a rosette shape without any help from anyone. The original mosaic variegate.

'Maggie May'
Double, frilled star of bright deep pink with a wide white edge. Heart-shaped, quilted, dark green leaves with a red back. Standard. M. Garford, African Violet Centre, England. This new hybrid from the Centre is of a striking colour that will be wanted for inclusion in the collection of many growers. Shapes and grows well.

'Ma Gigi'
Semi-double to double star of burgundy with bright pink fantasy spots and a darker edge. Quilted, ruffled, dark green leaves. Standard. D. Croteau, Canada. AVSA Reg. No. 7248. An interesting plant to grow that sometimes loses the pink fantasy spots on propagation.

'Magnolia'
Semi-double to double, light pink. Pointed, ovate, strawberry leaves of very dark green, almost black with a dark red back. Large. M. Burns, USA (from seed of R. Nadeau, USA). AVSA Reg. No. 6378. A spectacular and very large-growing hybrid that is easy to bring to show standard.

'Margaret Rose'
Semi-double, frilled, two-toned pink with crimson lobe tips. Serrated, medium green leaves variegated with a dark pink edge. Standard. Dornbusch, Australia. The edged variegation complements the flower colour. This hybrid has adapted well to UK conditions.

'Maria'
Single, frilled clear pink. Tailored, medium green leaves. Standard. African Violet Centre, England. Easy-to-grow window-sill plant with many flowers in bloom at any one time.

'Merci Beaucoup'
Semi-double, pure white that may sometimes be tinted with very pale pink. Quilted, serrated, dark green leaves. Standard. D. Croteau, Canada. AVSA Reg. No. 7039. A hybrid that flowers early and continues to do so for a very long time. Easy to grow and very rewarding.

'Ness' Hey Jude'
Single, fringed, non-dropping medium pink. Plain, dark green leaves with a red back. Standard. D. Ness, USA. AVSA Reg. No. 6271. An

attractive and very good window-sill plant. It is also a very good plant for breeding new hybrids.

'Norfolk Belle'
Single to semi-double bell-shaped deep pink with a fuchsia centre. Pointed, light to medium green leaves. Standard. African Violet Centre, England. A hybrid that is easy to grow into a flat show-standard plant.

'Nortex Razzmatazz Haven'
Semi-double to double, rose-pink with a darker fuchsia glitter edge. Slightly pointed, quilted, dark green leaves. Standard. B. Johnson, USA. A startlingly coloured floriferous hybrid that is easy to grow. A frequent winner at shows.

'Ode to Beauty'
Semi-double star of medium coral with narrow raspberry border and a white edge. Quilted, dark green leaves. Large. B. Johnson, USA. AVSA Reg. No. 7677. A winner! This is a must for the show table, and it definitely lives up to its name.

'Optimara Colorado'
Single, fringed, magenta red. Quilted, medium to dark green leaves. Holt-kamp, USA. AVSA Reg. No. 3152. From the family that gave us the 'Rhap-sodie' series, the violets in the 'Optimara' series are equally as good. 'Colorado' is a must for hybridists as it is a very good seed and pollen parent.

'Phantom Flash'
Semi-double, frilled, lavender and purple bicolour. Tailored, glossy medium green leaves. Boone, USA. AVSA Reg. No. 7065. An extremely floriferous hybrid, the many large infloresences are long lasting, and the plant shapes easily. It has won many show awards.

'Picasso'
Double-cupped light blue with white fantasy spots and splashes, and a darker blue edge together with a near-white lobe back. Plain, medium green leaves variegated with white and pink and having a silver-green back. Large. M. Tremblay, Canada. AVSA Reg. No. 6924. A hybrid that is difficult to describe, but, once seen in full flower, a 'must-have' in a collection. The variegation may change with different conditions but this should not deter a grower. It is a beautiful hybrid.

'Powwow'
Single to semi-double, dark red. Plain, medium green leaves, edge

variegated with cream. Standard. K. Stork, USA. AVSA Reg. No. 7708. A startling colour combination of flower and leaf, growing to a very flat symmetrical plant. Performs well on the show table.

'Quilting Bee'
Double, fringed, two-toned lilac shading to a silver-lavender edge. Quilted, glossy, medium green leaves. Standard. K. Stork, USA. AVSA Reg. No. 7268. Unusual flower colour, and an easy-to-grow hybrid.

'Radiance'
Semi-double to double star of medium pink with a darker eye. Ovate, quilted, medium to dark green leaves with a red back. Standard. M. Garford, African Violet Centre, England. A good window-sill plant, its many flowers standing well above its neat foliage.

'Rhapsodie Elfriede'
Single, bright blue. Plain, dark green leaves. Standard. Holtkamp, Germany. One of the first non-dropping single-flowered hybrids.

'Rhapsodie Mars'
Double star of red. Tailored, medium to dark green leaves. Standard. Holtkamp, Germany. One of the second 'Rhapsodie' series, all of which had star-shaped flowers.

'Rococo Anna (syn. 'Rococo Pink')
Double, deep pink. Round, girl-type leaves of dark green. Standard. This hybrid can be difficult to grow into a flat rosette because of its distinctly round leaf shape, but it grows well otherwise.

'Rococo Marianne' (syn. 'Rococo Blue')
Full double, dark blue. Round, girl-type leaves of dark green. Standard. The growth habit is similar to 'Rococo Anna'.

'Roseberry'
Semi-double to double, two-toned rose. Plain, dark green leaves variegated with pink. Large standard. I. Fredette, USA. AVSA Reg. No. 7533. A show stopper and winner every time, an easy grower. Has been grown for at least ten years but only registered in the past three.

'Sarah'
Single, ruffled, magenta-pink with a white edge. Tailored, medium green leaves. Standard. African Violet Centre, England. A very good

plant to grow on a window-sill as it does not grow over-large and is attractive in flower.

'Silver Jubilee'
Double, medium to dark blue geneva. Tailored, slightly quilted, medium green leaves. Standard. M. Garford, African Violet Centre, England. A good window-sill plant to grow under British conditions.

'Silver Milestone'
Single to semi-double, ruffled, magenta geneva. Quilted, medium green leaves. Standard. J. Hill, England. AVSA Reg. No. 5969. This hybrid was named for the Silver Jubilee of the Saintpaulia and Houseplant Society. A very good window-sill plant with an unusual flower colour.

'Snow Ballet'
Double white. Quilted, pointed, light green leaves. Large standard. Eyerdom, Granger Gardens, USA. AVSA Reg. No. 1219. Another very much loved old favourite. Despite its official size, it can be grown very large. It performs better in natural daylight than under artificial lighting.

'Steven Martin'
Semi-double to double star of methyl-violet bicolour. Strawberry-type, emerald green leaves. Standard. E. Fisher, Canada. One of the easy-to-grow plants from this hybridist.

'Suncoast Seabreeze'
Double, ruffled, white with a light blue edge. Slightly wavy emerald-green leaves. Standard. S. Williams, USA. A delicately pretty hybrid.

'Tie-Dyed'
Double, two-toned purple with a white edge. Tailored, dark green leaves. Standard. Eyerdom, Granger Gardens, USA. Most who see this hybrid in flower want to grow it for themselves. The colouring is eye-catching on a plant that grows easily.

'Tiger'
Semi-double, dark blue. Tailored, medium-green leaves variegated with white and pink. Large. I. Fredette, USA. AVSA Reg. No. 3433. This really large, older hybrid is still winning on the show table. It is not the easiest to grow, but can be spectacular.

'Tomahawk'
Semi-double to double, fluted, bright red. Tailored, dark green leaves.

Large. K. Stork, USA. AVSA Reg. No. 7269. One of the reddest reds to date, and floriferous. The dark green foliage makes a wonderful background for the vibrant red flowers.

'Tommie Lou'
Double, white with a light orchid centre. Quilted, dark green leaves, variegated with a white edge. Large. Oden, USA. AVSA Reg. No. 1744. The original of the 'Tommie Lou'-type variegation, and still as breathtaking as when first seen.

'Tomoko'
Double, peach pink with a thin red edge. Plain, glossy, dark green leaves with a red back. Standard. Eyerdom, Granger Gardens, USA. AVSA Reg. No. 6451. A very early-flowering hybrid and easy to grow into a good symmetrical plant.

'Tribute to Bill'
Semi-double, in shades of blue, lavender and purple. Pointed, quilted, dark green leaves with a red back. Standard. B. Johnson, USA. Alas, this great hybridizer is no longer with us. However, he has left us some magnificent hybrids. This one has been named to honour him, and it flowers early and heavily.

'Ultimate'
Semi-double to double, stars of deep coral with fuchsia overtones and fantasy splashed with deep blue. Round, slightly scalloped, medium green leaves. Standard. B. Johnson, USA. Another beautiful hybrid left to us by Bill which flowers heavily.

'Vampire's Kiss'
Semi-double to double, dark blood-red with black shading. Quilted, dark green leaves. Standard. G. Boone, USA. A well-named hybrid considering the colour of the flowers, of which there are very many on a mature plant.

'Windy Day'
Semi-double, ruffled star of medium blue with a white-green edge. Wavy, glossy dark green leaves with a red back. Large. Boone, USA. AVSA Reg. No. 7719. A floriferous hybrid with good leaf-shaping qualities. A nice show plant.

'Wrangler's Dixie Celebration'
Semi-double, pink flowers of large size. Ruffled, medium green leaves

variegated with pink on the edge. Large. W. Smith, USA. AVSA Reg. No. 4490. A large-growing, superb show plant that never lets you down.

'Wrangler's Spanish Cavalier'
Semi-double, frilled, bright red-violet with a green and white edge. Glossy longifolia, medium green leaves, variegated with pink and a hint of bronze. Large. W. Smith, USA. AVSA Reg. No. 6235. A show stopper with a wonderful colour combination.

'Zonta'
Semi-double to double bright pink. Very slightly wavy, dark green leaves with a red back. Standard. H. Pittman, USA. AVSA Reg. No. 5194. A heavily and continually flowering hybrid that grows easily to a symmetrical rosette. A good plant for a beginner.

MINIATURE OR SEMI-MINIATURE HYBRIDS

'Bahamian Sunset'
Double burgundy with white tips to the lobes. Pointed, strawberry type, dark green leaves. Miniature. Brownlie, Canada. AVSA Reg. No. 4604. A hybrid that grows easily into a floriferous small posy.

'Chantamara'
Full double, white. Tailored, heart-shaped, light to medium green leaves. Miniature. From Holland. A delightful miniature with many small powder-puff flowers.

'Chantinge'
Single to semi-double, dark coral. Tailored, glossy medium to dark green leaves with a red back. Miniature. From Holland. A striking colour combination of flowers and foliage.

'Chantora'
Single, glowing deep red. Pointed, very dark green leaves with a deep red back. Miniature. From Holland. Outstanding colour combination of flower and leaf. Easy-to-grow, single-crowned plant.

'Crushed Velvet'
Semi-double, frilled burgundy. Tailored, dark green leaves. Semi-miniature. G. Boone, USA. The flower colour is outstanding, and the plant well named.

'Dizzy Lizzy'
Semi-double, dark pink with dark blue fantasy markings. Pointed, medium green leaves variegated with white. Semi-miniature. Lyon/ Sorano, USA. AVSA Reg. No. 6351. Not entirely reliable as to colour pattern, hence the name. Even so, a very rewarding plant to grow.

'Hand Made'
Semi-double, dark purple. Serrated, medium to dark green leaves vari- egated with white. Semi-miniature. H. Pittman, USA. AVSA Reg. No. 7380. Grows to a symmetrical leaf pattern easily.

'Irish Angel'
Double, light blue with a green edge. Plain, pointed, medium green leaves. Semi-miniature. L. Egenites, USA. AVSA Reg. No. 4054. Un- usually shaped flowers in that the lobes are cupped up and so do not open fully; even so, it is an attractive little plant.

'Jolita'
Full double, lavender pink. Tailored, medium green leaves with a pink back. Miniature. From Holland. The powder-puff flowers nearly cover the foliage, making a very floriferous little plant.

'Little Katherine'
Semi-double white. Pointed, heart-shaped, glossy medium green leaves. Semi-miniature. A. Hart, USA. AVSA Reg. No. 6238. A little darling that has done a great deal of winning in competitive shows.

'Little Pro'
Semi-double, light pink. Pointed, quilted, shiny, dark green leaves with deep red back. Semi-miniature. H. Pittman, USA. AVSA Reg. No. 6637. Without any effort on the grower's part, this hybrid will become a lovely symmetrical show plant.

'Little Stormy'
Double, dark blue. Plain, glossy, dark green leaves variegated with pink and white. Semi-miniature. Lyndon Lyon Greenhouses, USA. An aptly named hybrid that is easy to grow.

'Midget Valentine'
Single, fuchsia red. Plain, glossy, medium green, crown-variegated leaves with white. Miniature. E. Champion, USA. AVSA Reg. No. 2524. An early, crown-variegated miniature. Still being entered in competitive shows and winning.

'Nicky'
Full double, frilled, medium pink. Wavy, glossy medium green leaves. Semi-miniature. From Holland. A delight to grow. The flowers and foliage complement one another.

'Novita'
Single, medium to dark blue. Tailored, medium green leaves. Miniature. From Holland. Many comparatively large flowers cover the flat-growing rosette foliage.

'Optimara Little Sapphire'
Single, light blue two-tone. Plain, medium green leaves. Miniature. Holtkamp, USA. AVSA Reg. No. 6566. An easy-to-grow, miniature hybrid that makes a pretty display.

'Optimara Rose Quartz'
Single to semi-double, pink. Pointed, ovate, glossy, medium green leaves. Miniature. Holtkamp, USA. AVSA Reg. No. 6969. Probably the best Optimara miniature in this series of gem-stone names. Seldom without a flower.

'Pat Champagne'
Semi-double, dark blue with a white edge. Ovate, dark green leaves variegated with cream. Semi-miniature. H. Pittman, USA. AVSA Reg. No. 7084. An interesting, flat-growing hybrid that is a consistent winner at shows in the USA.

'Playful Pet'
Single, stick-tight dark rose. Plain, dark green leaves. Semi-miniature. H. Pittman, USA. An easy grower. Flowers and shapes well.

'Precious Pink'
Semi-double pink. Plain, medium green leaves with 'Tommie Lou' variegation of pink. Semi-miniature. H. Pittman, USA. AVSA Reg. No. 6025. This is a precious hybrid and is almost guaranteed to win at shows, even to beat much larger-growing African violets as 'Best in Show'.

'Reggi'
Double, light blue with a white edge. Tailored, pointed, medium green leaves with a red back. Miniature. From Holland. This hybrid is easy to grow and is very floriferous, making a good display.

'Rob's Angelie'
Double, frilled white with a rose-pink shaded edge. Tailored, glossy,

medium green leaves. Miniature. Ralph Robinson, USA. AVSA Reg. No. 7557. A pretty little floriferous hybrid with comparatively large flowers.

'Rob's Bedazzled'
Double, lavender mauve with a white geneva edge. Pointed, slightly serrated, medium to dark green leaves variegated with white and with a dark red back. Miniature. Ralph Robinson, USA. AVSA Reg. No. 6470. A very heavy flowerer that grows into a symmetrical posy easily.

'Rob's Copper Cat'
Semi-double, fringed copper pink with dark green edge. Wavy, very dark green leaves with 'Tommie Lou' variegation of copper pink and a red back. Semi-miniature. R. Robinson, USA. AVSA Reg. No. 7030. An outstanding and unusual combination of colour and shape. A good grower.

'Rob's Dandy Lion'
Semi-double, bell-shaped, pewter-silver with distinct yellow anthers. Tailored, nearly black-green leaves variegated with white. Semi-miniature. Ralph Robinson, USA. AVSA Reg. No. 7731. An unusual colour combination and grows well.

'Rob's Little Butterfly'
Semi-double to double, light pink. Tailored, serrated, dark green leaves with a red back. Semi-miniature. Ralph Robinson, USA. The rosette-growing foliage is often hidden by the comparatively large flowers.

'Rob's Sandstorm'
Double, light blue with heavily splashed fantasy of dark purple. Pointed dark green leaves variegated with white and with a dark red back. Miniature. Ralph Robinson, USA. AVSA Reg. No. 7035. A heavily flowering hybrid, and like all Rob's', a good grower and show plant.

'Rob's Violet Sky'
Double, dark wine-purple. Pointed, dark green leaves, crown-variegated with cream and tan and a red back. Semi-miniature. R. Robinson, USA. AVSA Reg. No. 7439. The flowers form a halo of colour around the crown variegation.

'Shan'
Double, dark blue-purple with an occasional white edge to the lobes. Pointed, black-green leaves. Miniature. B. Johnson, USA. A very pleasing hybrid from the master hybridizer.

'Snuggles'

Semi-double pink. Tailored, medium green leaves with 'Tommie Lou' variegation of white. Semi-miniature. Lyndon Lyon Greenhouses, USA. AVSA Reg. No. 5018. First of the 'Snuggles' series which are all easy to grow.

'Snuggles Lady Dawn'

Semi-double, star of pink with mauve markings on tips. Heart-shaped, serrated, girl, medium green leaves variegated with white. Semi-miniature. Sorano, USA. AVSA Reg. No. 7602. Easy growing, flat girl foliage and many flowers.

'Snuggles Rising Star'

Semi-double, wavy star of light pink with a rose-pink overlay and a pink to white edge. Plain, medium green leaves variegated with white. Semi-miniature. Sorano, USA. AVSA Reg. No. 7604. The many fairly large flowers make this a very attractive hybrid with its 'Tommie Lou' variegated foliage.

'Socket Toomey'

Semi-double star of pink, with purple fantasy splashes. Tailored, slightly serrated, light green leaves. Semi-miniature. Neff, USA. This hybrid is worth growing if only for its name. It has a tendency at times to lose its purple splashes.

'Teen Sweetheart'

Semi-double, medium blue with a white edge. Plain, medium green leaves variegated with white. Semi-miniature. H. Pittman, USA. AVSA Reg. No. 7867. A sweetheart of a hybrid. Grows and flowers well.

'Wee Dear'

Semi-double, medium pink. Pointed, medium green leaves, 'Tommie Lou' variegated with white. Miniature. H. Pittman, USA. AVSA Reg. No. 6255. A pretty little hybrid, well worth growing as it is an easy one.

TRAILING HYBRIDS

'Cambridge Wanderer'

Semi-double pink with a darker edge. Plain, medium green leaves, variegated with white and pink. Semi-miniature trailer. A.E. Adams, Canada. Medium-length growth that makes a neat plant.

'Daisy Trail'

Double, narrow-lobed white with prominent yellow anthers. Pointed, heart-shaped, light green leaves. Standard trailer. African Violet Centre, England. This hybrid, after much propagation, now has blue intermixed with the white in the flower. A good sturdy trailer.

'Dancin' Trail'

Double star of red. Pointed, glossy dark green leaves with a dark red back. Semi-miniature. S. Sorano, USA. AVSA Reg. No. 5565. Produces masses of flowers which almost cover the foliage. An easy grower, and often wins.

'Ding Dong Trail'

Single, bell-shaped pink with a darker eye. Pointed, medium green leaves. Standard trailer. African Violet Centre, England. A well-named and vigorous grower; it makes a good basket plant.

'Fancy Trail'

Double, pink. Tailored, emerald-green leaves variegated with yellow and sometimes pink. Standard trailer. Lyon, USA. AVSA Reg. No. 3674. A good trailing hybrid with very many smallish flowers of a shade that stands out against the variegated foliage.

'Glitter Fountain'

Semi-double pink with a red glitter edge and red fantasy speckles. Tailored, dark green leaves, crown-variegated with cream and pink. Standard trailer. I. Fredette, USA. A recent introduction with a fine colour combination and growth.

'Honeysuckle Rose'

Double, rose pink. Heart-shaped, light green leaves variegated with cream and yellow. Standard trailer. Dattalo, USA. AVSA Reg. No. 6255. An attractive hybrid with a good trailing habit.

'Jet Trail'

Double, wisteria blue. Slightly serrated and pointed medium green leaves. Semi-miniature trailer. Lyndon Lyon, USA. If only one trailing hybrid can be grown in a collection, this is the one! It is a floriferous plant, easy to shape.

'Magic Trail'

Semi-double, star of pale pink. Pointed, quilted, medium green leaves. Standard trailer. African Violet Centre, England. Trails well over a pot rim and has many flowers.

'Meteor Trail'
Double, red. Tailored, dark green leaves. Standard trailer. African Violet Centre, England. We consider this to be the nicest of the Centre's trailers to date. It trails well, flowers well and the colour combination is good.

'Midnight Trail'
Double star of medium blue. Tailored, light green leaves. Standard trailer. African Violet Centre, England. Another good trailing hybrid with plenty of flowers.

'Milky Way Trail'
Single to semi-double, white. Heart-shaped, quilted medium green leaves. Semi-miniature trailer. J. Stahl, USA. AVSA Reg. No. 7169. The small white flowers cover this well-named hybrid which is fairly easy to grow.

'Moonlight Trail'
Double, pale blue. Pointed, medium green leaves. Standard trailer. African Violet Centre, England. Another hybrid from the Centre that is floriferous and trails well.

'Ombrelle'
Semi-double to double, light pink. Tailored, heart-shaped, medium green leaves. Semi-miniature trailer. M. Tremblay, Canada. Flowers long and well. Often the foliage is completely covered with flowers.

'Orchid Trail'
Double, orchid red. Heart-shaped, glossy dark green leaves. Semi-miniature trailer. H. Pittman, USA. An extremely floriferous trailer, the foliage is hidden beneath the great many glowing flowers.

'Pip Squeek'
Single, bell-shaped star of pale pink. Tiny, pointed, dark green leaves. Micro-miniature semi-trailer. Lyndon Lyon, USA. AVSA Reg. No. 3603. A very popular plant amongst the collectors of these minute hybrids.

'Pixie Blue'
Single, deep blue. Plain, ovate medium to dark green leaves. Miniature trailer. Lyon, USA. AVSA Reg. No. 2598. An old hybrid that still performs and competes with today's hybrids. An easy grower that will give great pleasure.

'Pixie Trail'
Single, pink with a darker eye. Small, round, medium green leaves.

Miniature semi-trailer. Lyon, USA. A hybrid with short branching stems. The same age as 'Pixie Blue' and just as floriferous and easy growing.

'Ramblin' Dots'
Double star of light lavender with light purple fantasy. Plain, light green leaves variegated with white and yellow. Standard trailer. Sorano, USA. AVSA Reg. No. 6360. Fast-growing and freely flowering hybrid. One for the collection.

'Rob's Sailor Bill'
Double pale pink with a darker eye. Pointed medium green leaves. Semi-miniature trailer. Ralph Robinson, USA. Shapes well as a trailer with plenty of flower.

'Rob's Sticky Wicket'
Semi-double, medium fuchsia. Pointed, medium green leaves. Semi-miniature trailer. Ralph Robinson, USA. AVSA Reg. No. 6467. A very easy-to-grow hybrid that does not have to be encouraged to branch and trail. A very floriferous show winner.

'Sky Trail'
Semi-double to double, blue with a white edge. Plain, medium green leaves. Standard trailer. E. Fisher, Canada. A very good, old hybrid with an abundance of beautiful blue flowers.

'Snowy Trail'
Double, white with at times a pink tinge. Pointed, light green leaves. Semi-miniature trailer. Lyon, USA. AVSA Reg. No. 3678. An old favourite trailer that still performs well and still competes with modern trailers.

'Sprite'
Single, white that can have a hint of blue in the centre. Heart-shaped, light green leaves. Micro-miniature semi-trailer. African Violet Centre, England. Readily makes short branching growth. Best grown in a shallow pan rather than in a pot.

'Starry Trail'
Semi-double to double, narrow-lobed white. Tailored, dark green leaves. Standard trailer. African Violet Centre, England. A vigorous trailer with glistening flowers.

'Trails Away'
Double, dark orchid pink. Plain, medium green leaves. Standard trailer.

Lyndon Lyon, USA. An older hybrid which can still be seen in collections, and grows and trails well.

'Violet Trail'
Single star of amethyst mauve. Tailored, serrated, dark green leaves with a velvety sheen and a red back. Standard trailer. Lyndon Lyon, USA. AVSA Reg. No. 2468. A very early trailer that really lives up to its trailing habit. A rather shy bloomer, but the beauty of the foliage makes up for the lack of flowers; these are also beautiful.

CHIMERA HYBRIDS

'Amanda'
Single pink with a central red stripe. Round, dark green leaves. Standard. From Holland. This hybrid should be a success growing on a window-sill as well as under lights.

'Inge-Clara'
Single, white with medium purple central stripe. Tailored, dark green leaves with a pink back. Standard. From Holland. A recent introduction. Apparently a good window-sill plant.

'Kiwi Dazzle'
Single, fringed red with a white central stripe. Tailored, medium green leaves. Standard. Snell, New Zealand. AVSA Reg. No. 5888. An easy-to-grow chimera.

'Little Seagull'
Single, white with a dark blue central stripe. Plain, pointed, medium green leaves. Semi-miniature trailer. Savage, USA. AVSA Reg. No. 5989. Rather floriferous, but has a tendency to drop its flowers. Otherwise a pretty plant.

'Mauna Loa'
Single, slightly cupped star of rose coral with a deep red orchid central stripe. Pointed, dark green leaves and a red back. Large standard. Hugh Eyerdom, Granger Gardens, USA. AVSA Reg. No. 5336. A very striking, large-growing plant.

'Myrthe'
Single, fringed white with cerise central stripe. Quilted, medium green leaves. Standard. From Holland. A recent introduction that should grow well on a window-sill.

'Ness' Mini Sota'

Single, very pale blush pink with a bright fuchsia pink central stripe. Slightly scalloped, light green leaves. Semi-miniature. Ness, USA. AVSA Reg. No. 7647. A small plant which performs well.

'Pony Ride'

Single, bell-shaped white with a narrow striped edge of medium blue. Plain medium green leaves. Miniature trailer. Sorano, USA. AVSA Reg. No. 7590. An exquisite little hybrid with tiny bell flowers.

'Rob's Magnetic Field'

Double, deep pink with a dark blue central stripe. Girl-type dark green leaves with a red back. Miniature. R. Robinson, USA. AVSA Reg. No. 7033. An interesting plant to grow, needing a little more attention due to the girl foliage.

'Red Mt. Fuji'

Single, bright rose with a deep fuchsia central stripe. Tailored, pointed, quilted dark green leaves. Standard. Horikoshi and Kawakami, Japan. AVSA Reg. No. 7812. A mutant of the hybrid 'Mt. Fuji', a nice symmetrical grower.

'Silk Reflection'

Double, ruffled star of pink with a lavender blue central stripe. Plain, slightly wavy, medium green leaves lightly 'Tommie Lou' variegated with white. Large standard. J. Wells, USA. AVSA Reg. No. 6341. A striking chimera hybrid when well grown.

'Tineka'

Single, medium pink with a mauve central stripe. Tailored, dark green leaves with a red back. Standard. A recent introduction from Holland. A compact, symmetrical plant.

'Victorian Ribbons'

Semi-double, frilled, reddish wine-purple with a central white stripe. Tailored, medium green leaves variegated with white. Standard. Sorano, USA. Clusters of flowers nearly cover the foliage to make a striking hybrid.

TOWARDS YELLOW FLOWERS

'Golden Threads'

Semi-double to double stars of white, streaked and blushed with very pale yellow in varying amounts. Tailored, medium green leaves. Standard. Sorano, USA. AVSA Reg. No. 7957. Released in 1993.

'His Promise'
Full double, white with a hint of very pale primrose yellow and at times a blush of pink. Tailored, medium green leaves. Standard. Blansit, USA. Released at the AVSA Convention 1992. The flower colour can be a little unstable.

'Majesty'
Double, slightly frilled white, shaded and streaked with very pale yellow and pink. Wavy, serrated, medium green leaves. Standard. Blansit, USA. Released at the AVSA Convention 1992. The shading and streaking can be variable, but the plant shapes well.

'Playful Dreamer'
Semi-double, frilled soft pink, shaded with ivory and streaked with very pale yellow. Tailored, very dark green, almost black, leaves. Standard. Sorano, USA. AVSA Reg. No. 7983. Released in 1993. A good symmetrically growing posy with a colour that is different.

These hybrids are the early breakthrough to yellow African violet flowers. The degree of yellowness depends upon the culture and conditions they are given and the maturity of the plants. They appear to require cooler temperatures, less feeding and less intensity of light. They grow well on window-sills for these reasons, and the yellow coloration intensifies as the plant reaches maturity and ages.

At present there are no hybrids with flowers of a solid, deep yellow colour; that is likely to come in the future.

4

CULTIVATION

We cannot count the number of times we have heard someone say, 'I cannot grow African violets'. We would like to tell all these disappointed people that African violets are comparatively easy to grow, and we would like to encourage them to try again. By using the methods we shall explain in the following pages they should have some success. There is nothing mystical about growing African violets, as we have found during the many years we have been obsessed by them!

The important factors to consider are light, temperature, compost, pots, correct watering, humidity and feeding.

LIGHT

All plants require a good intensity of light to grow and produce flowers. The action of light upon the chlorophyll in green-leaved plants converts, by the chemical process of photosynthesis, water, carbon dioxide and fertilizers into sugar foodstuffs that the plants can use for growth. Different plant genera require different light intensities, and therefore one must consider the conditions of their original habitat to be able to provide them with light of somewhat similar intensity.

Although African violets originated in East Africa close to the equator and therefore in the tropics, their natural habitat was in rocky areas near water shaded by trees and not in open, intensely sunny situations. Another point to remember is that at the equator, day and night are of equal length and so African violets require periods of light and dark during twenty-four hours.

Knowing all this, we can safely say that during the summer months they require the intensity of bright diffused light, but not direct hot sunshine; in fact when exposed to the latter the foliage of the plant becomes exceedingly pale, stunted in growth, shrivelled and burned, so that the plant ultimately dies. One way to assess the light intensity falling on a plant in summer is to hold one's hand between the plant and the sunlight and then to look at its shadow on the plant. If the shadow is clearly defined, the sunlight is too strong and the intensity too high, in which case the plant should be moved to another, shadier position. If the shadow of the hand can just be seen, the light intensity is just right.

During the winter months, the light intensity of the sun is greatly reduced so that in northern latitudes African violets may be fully exposed to it and not be harmed in any way. In fact in these latitudes the light intensity is not sufficiently adequate nor of a long enough daily period to promote budding, and so African violets are said to rest. It is possible to increase daylight length in winter with the use of fluorescent light tubes; this is explained more fully below.

Position in the Home
Any reduction in light intensity is not appreciated by the human eye as much as it is by plants; thus what appears to us as a bright position in a room may well seem to be very dark to a plant. From this it can be understood that although a table in the centre of a room is a good position for *us* to enjoy a flowering African violet, it is not the place for it to stay for more than a week without it losing some of its beauty; any leaves and flowers will pale, and budding will cease. Remember that light intensity falling on a plant at a window is reduced by about 50 per cent when that plant is moved about 2ft (60cm) in from that window.

Therefore when growing African violet plants on a window-sill, they should be placed as close to the glass as possible during the daytime. Early morning and early evening direct sunlight are not detrimental to African violets, and so plants may be kept safely on east- or west-facing window-sills all the year round. However south-facing windows, or any that get full summer sunshine, should be avoided if at all possible unless shaded by a tree outside to give filtered light. Otherwise either a thick net curtain should hang between the glass and the plant, or the plant should be brought further into the room during the hottest period of the day and then returned to the window-sill in the late afternoon. In winter, however, south-facing window-sills generally prove to be a good position for African violets, as any sunlight there is at that time of year will be beneficial. Windows of northern aspect provide a good position in the hot summer months, but not during winter, as these window-sills are then much colder and do not have a long enough daylight period to sustain the plants.

Whenever plants are grown on window-sills they should be turned by a quarter turn each day in order that they grow evenly, straight upright. If this is not done, the leaves on the side of the plant furthest away from the window will grow reaching for the light, and the whole plant will end up growing at an angle, leaning towards the window.

Growing under Fluorescent Lighting
It may not be realized that given adequate conditions of light, African violets are capable of flowering all the year round. These conditions may

be achieved by using artificial light, of which the best source is a fluorescent tube with a light emission equating closely to the intensity of natural sunlight. The spectrum of the latter contains all wavelengths from far red through orange to green to far blue, all of which are either reflected or absorbed by plants. We see plant foliage as green because the yellow and green wavelengths are reflected back by the leaves as little used, whereas red and blue wavelengths are absorbed by the leaves and used in photosynthesis and other growth reactions.

Fluorescent tubes are normally termed 'warm white' and 'daylight' or 'cool white'. Experience has shown that a fluorescent tube fitment holding one warm white tube and one daylight tube, alongside each other but 6 to 9in (15 to 23cm) apart, give the intensity and type of light that produce good growth in African violets. There are also fluorescent tubes made for horticultural use which appear pink or blue in colour to us when lit. These can give an increase in growth level, although for the amateur this particular increase does not really merit the extra cost, which is at least twice as much as the cost of warm white tubes. Today there are also low-energy tubes available which can be fitted into a light system; these give good light intensity and useful wavelengths using less electricity.

By comparison with fluorescent light, incandescent light – such as that from household light bulbs – produces a great deal more heat, it is not as useful a light spectrum, and such bulbs are much more expensive to run. However, in the winter months a plant that normally lives on a windowsill will benefit from a few extra hours of light when placed under a lighted table lamp during the evening.

The best way of using fluorescent lighting for African violets is to have it fitted either in individually shelved plant stands, or under shelves built into a dark corner in a room. Open-fronted bookcases may also be utilized, providing their shelves are of an adequate size to hold plants without crushing the leaves, and are far enough apart for the foliage and flowers not to be damaged by being too close to the tubes.

Shelves housing standard-sized plants should be about 2ft (60cm) apart so that the fluorescent tubes are approximately 18in (45cm) above the plant foliage. When growing miniature hybrids, the distance between tubes and foliage should be reduced to about 6in (15cm). This can be achieved by raising the miniature plants, placing them on upturned pots or something similar of a suitable height, and is relevant if a mixture of African violet plants of different sizes are being grown together on the same shelf.

The best distance to maintain between fluorescent tubes and each type of plant must be found by experiment. The plants themselves will tell you whether or not they are happy with the distance between them and the

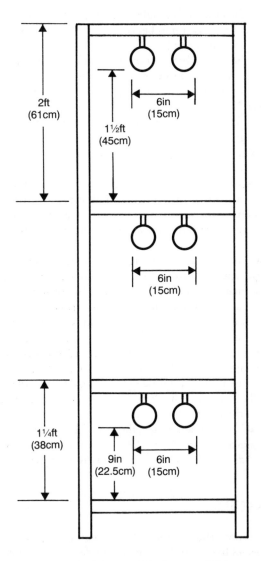

2ft
(61cm)

1½ft
(45cm)

6in
(15cm)

6in
(15cm)

1¼ft
(38cm)

9in
(22.5cm)

6in
(15cm)

End view of outline of three-shelf plant stand for fluorescent lighting.

tubes: their leaves will turn down to hug the pot if they are too close to the light, or they will reach up towards the light when it is too far away.

For optimum growth, fluorescent lighting should be switched on for a period of twelve to fourteen hours a day, or for a maximum of sixteen hours, because African violets grown under artificial light must have a

minimum of eight hours of complete darkness. Again, only by experiment can you find the exact number of hours of light to give, in order to
achieve the best growth results.

It should also be noted that light intensity differs along the length of a
fluorescent tube. With this in mind, African violets with light-coloured
flowers and leaves should be positioned towards the tube ends as they
require a lower light intensity than dark-coloured flowers and leaves;
these latter should be placed towards the centre of the tube length.
Variegated foliage plants should also be positioned centrally, as their
optimum growth is encouraged there whether they are light or dark
coloured.

When fluorescent tubes need replacing, only one should be changed at
a time, and with a week or two between. This is because new tubes have
a high light intensity for several days when first used, and if both were
replaced at the same time this would bleach the colour from the plants
beneath them.

Plants grown under fluorescent lighting should stand on watertight
trays fitted with capillary matting for ease of movement; gravel would be
too heavy. The matting should be kept moist to create humidity (see p.
62). It is advisable that all electrical fitting is carried out by a qualified
electrician: everyone knows that electricity and water do not mix.

The real African violet enthusiast will convert a room in his house
solely for growing his favourite houseplant under lights, with all the
controllers for light, heat and ventilation. Our American friends often
convert the basement of their house for growing plants, and this is something we greatly envy since in Britain, houses with basements are very
much a thing of the past.

Fluorescent tubes are made in lengths from 1ft (30cm) to 8ft (240cm),
and obviously a grower will choose the most suitable length for his shelv-
ing. A rough guide for the wattage of a tube is 10 watts per foot length.

TEMPERATURE

Although equatorial, African violets do not require tropical temperatures
since all the species have their habitats at altitudes up to 4,000ft (1,200m),
and so are actually growing in cooler temperatures.

We have found that the best temperature range for good growth is 65–
75°F (18–24°C) during the daytime, with a night-time drop of 10°F
(5°C). During the summer months, high temperatures can be a great
problem and a period of four or five days at a temperature of 85°F (29°C)
and over will almost certainly prove fatal to African violets. It may be
helpful to increase the levels of humidity and ventilation. Then during the

winter months the problem shifts to too cold a temperature: whilst an African violet will just survive a short period at 55°F (13°C) by ceasing to grow, once the temperature falls below 50°F (10°C) the plant will collapse and die. It is advisable during such cold spells to reduce watering in order to prevent damage to the roots as much as possible.

In summer, open windows will provide air circulation that will normally control room temperature somewhat; it is only when excessively hot weather lasts for a week or more that African violets suffer heat exhaustion and collapse. In this situation there is very little that can be done, other than to keep the air moving by using an electric fan or air conditioning equipment. Centrally heated homes in winter give the warmth needed to keep plants in good order, provided that the heating is not turned off overnight. However, it must be emphasized that plants should not be left on windowsills behind drawn curtains, because even if the windows are double glazed, it will still be much too cold for them overnight.

COMPOST

Most of the African violet species were found growing among rocks in very little soil, and this was composed mainly of humus. From this is can be understood why the root system is shallow, with hair-like roots, and why it requires an easily draining compost.

Over the years many types of compost have been used, and it is for the grower to find the compost which is most suitable for growing African violets in the conditions provided. One very important fact to remember is that whatever the growing mixture, ideally its pH value should be between 6.7 and 7.0.

Understanding pH

Problems develop rapidly in the growing of African violets once pH values extend beyond the ideal range, and the problems become severe the further away the value is from the ideal. The effect on plants of the pH value being either too low or too high is the same, in that the rate of growth will be much slower and therefore mature plants will not grow to their full potential in size and flower, and the foliage will lack its normal lustre. The main reason for these effects is that essential nutritional elements will be locked up in the compost so that the root system is unstable to fulfil its function of absorbing them.

The pH value of a growing medium expresses the percentage concentrations of hydrogen (H^+) ions and hydroxyl (OH^-) ions in solution, and there is an arbitrary scale of pH from 1.0 which is extremely acidic, to 14.0 which is extremely alkaline. An increase in the percentage of hydrogen ions increases the acidity of the solution, and an increased percentage of hydroxyl ions gives an increase in alkalinity. When the percentage concentrations are equal, the solution is neutral, and this is pH 7.0 which is the mid-point of the scale. What is probably not understood is that one unit of pH is ten times that of the unit above it. In other words, at pH 5.0 the acidity is ten times the acidity at pH 6.0, and that at pH 4.0 is ten times that at pH 5.0. The scale is similar on the alkaline side of neutral.

Excessive acidity or alkalinity has a detrimental effect on the beneficial micro-organisms, or bacteria, by reducing their populations in the compost so that they cannot convert the essential nutritional elements into a form that the plant roots can absorb for growth. To avoid much of this problem, standard and large-sized show African violets should be root pruned and repotted every six months, and miniature and semi-miniature plants every three to four months.

Correcting pH Value in a Compost

Fresh potting compost should always be of the correct pH value, and if it is not, then correction should be made. A compost which is too acidic, below pH 6.6, may be improved by adding to the potting mixture dolomitic lime containing magnesium carbonate, rather than calcium carbonate – although dolomitic lime does contain some of the latter compound. Ordinary garden lime contains very high amounts of calcium compounds, and so should not be used as it will completely burn the root system, thus killing the plant. Too alkaline a compost can be corrected by watering the plant with a solution consisting of one teaspoon (5ml) of distilled white vinegar to one gallon (4.5 litres) of water. This process is obviously a slow method of correction as it is carried out on a potted plant. Also for correcting alkalinity there are pelleted, slow-release sulphur chips now available; these can be crushed so as to incorporate them evenly into a batch of compost before it is used.

Whichever way the correction is made, whether from too acid or too alkaline, the pH value should always be checked frequently using a meter during the correction.

The Constituents of Compost

There are many commercial compost mixes, usually based on peat or peat substitutes, and these have proved successful in use for many growers. However, some people prefer not to use ready-mixed commercial composts but to make up their own mix. For these we now explain the properties of the various constituents that may be used.

Peat The best type to use is sphagnum moss peat; it is long stranded so makes an open medium when used alone. Over a period of time it will break down and become too acidic for good plant growth, therefore repotting into fresh peat will be required fairly frequently. Garden or sedge peat is much finer in composition, coming from a grass as it does, and it readily compacts in use. It is also much more acidic, and correction of the pH value would be required before use. Peat has no food value, and plants would need feeding from the time of potting.

Coir This peat substitute is produced from coconut fibre and has been used with varying success for growing African violets. It usually has a neutral pH value of 7.0, although at times it has been known to have a pH of 5.3, and so it should always be checked before use. Like peat it contains no nutrients and therefore plants would need to be fed from when they are first potted. Coir is preferred to peat by environmentalists as it is produced from a renewable source, coconuts being an important world crop.

Bark There are several grades of bark that may be used as a growing medium. For African violets the pulverized grade should be used, although at times this may be a little powdery. It is often used with other constituents in compost mixtures. Again, always check its pH value before use.

Loam Loam-based composts can rarely be used on their own for growing African violets because they tend to compact in use so that the plant's fine root system cannot penetrate their mass. Normally loam has an alkaline pH of 7.5 and above which would deter good growth of African violets. Any loam used in a mixture should be pasteurized before use.

Pasteurization It is always advisable to pasteurize any peat, peat substitute medium or loam before use to kill any harmful organisms, insect pests and weed seeds that may be present. This can be done by heating the moist medium in a closed pan in an oven at 180–195°F (85–90°C) for thirty to forty-five minutes. It should then be stored in a closed container for two days before use so that any beneficial bacteria that may have been set back in numbers can re-establish themselves.

Pasteurizing is not sterilizing, which is steam heating in excess of 212°F (100°C) for a similar period and would eradicate all the beneficial bacteria present. Ready-mixed commercial composts should also be pasteurized, especially if your local garden centres keep their stock uncovered in the open. The unwanted organisms that can penetrate the packaging of composts can be surprising.

Horticultural Vermiculite This sterile medium is a mica mineral that has been exfoliated, or expanded, by being heated to a very high temperature. It contains no food value. The spongy pieces are made up of individual plates of mica which hold water between them. It is most useful as a course grade material to open up composts, and very much less useful as a fine grade because of its propensity to break down into individual plates which have no water retention properties. Always use horticultural grades of vermiculite, as other grades are used for insulation and these are not cleaned and so will contain substances harmful to plants.

Perlite This is a white lava rock which has been expanded by treatment involving great heat. It has excellent water retention properties, and is also used to open up a compost mix. It is advisable to wet perlite before using it, because the dust caused from minute fragments breaking away from the larger particles can be an irritant to some people, especially those suffering chest problems. Perlite is also a sterile medium and without any food value.

Horticultural Sharp Sand The most useful type is river-washed sand. It does not retain water, and is used solely as a compost opener to increase drainage; there are various grain sizes, and a coarse grade will give good drainage. Sand from the beach should never be used, as no matter how much it is washed it will always contain salt and other harmful substances.

Other Constituents Charcoal may also be included in small amounts in a home-made compost mixture. It is known as 'a sweetener' because it is able to absorb certain unwanted vapours from the mixture. Wood charcoal pieces about 0.25in (0.75cm) square are a good size to include.

A balanced fertilizer also needs to be incorporated in any made-up compost mixture that has no food value – although by far the best for African violets is to use a soluble fertilizer when watering; then there is no risk of root burn.

Compost Mixtures
Various recipes are in use, as everyone has his own favourite. However, a good general mixture for African violets is one part sphagnum moss peat or peat substitute, to one part vermiculite or perlite; use a 4in (10cm) pot, for example, as a measure. This mixture has no nutrients in it and therefore soluble fertilizers should be given to the plants from when they are first potted.

Another recipe uses one part by volume each of peat and sharp sand, the latter providing extra weight for pot stability especially when using plastic pots. This mixture also requires soluble fertilizers to be fed, right from the start of potting.

Loam-based compost may also be used as a constitutent in a potting mixture of one part loam-based, two parts sphagnum moss peat, and one part vermiculite or perlite. This recipe has the advantage that feeding is not needed until about four weeks after potting because of the nutrients in the loam. The alkalinity of the latter is lessened by the acidity of the peat, but the pH value should be checked on mixing.

Plants grown on a wick-watering system (*see* page 58) may need a compost containing a higher proportion of perlite in order that it does not become over-wet, even though perlite retains water. An example of such a mixture is one part sphagnum moss peat, one part vermiculite and two parts perlite, all by volume. Before using any home-made compost mixture always check that its pH value is between 6.7 and 7.0, and correct if necessary.

It is by experimenting with various recipes that the best compost mixture for one's own growing conditions can be found. When experimenting, for whatever reason, work with only two or three plants at a time; never change an entire routine for the whole collection until good results are known.

The authors' preferred compost mixture, after many years of growing African violets, is two parts by volume of a commercial peat-based compost, to one part vermiculite and one part perlite for general growing; the amount of perlite is altered for certain stages of growth of the plants. For example, as a plant reaches maturity the amount of perlite is reduced. The preferred compost is a mixture of sphagnum moss peat and vermiculite together with slow-release fertilizers; it is supplied dry so that the fertilizers do not begin to release until moistened for potting. As this sort of compost is often sold only in 100-litre bags it is essential that it is stored in dry conditions, so it remains in the condition in which it is sold. Although this may seem an overlarge quantity to buy at a time, it remains perfectly good for use over at least a two–year period.

When this sort of commercial compost is needed for potting, it is a good plan to add the water to it the day before it is wanted so that it is at the correct, even moistness throughout for potting. If it is used as soon as it is wetted, plant roots can be damaged by being in contact with patches of over-wet and over-dry compost.

POTS

As regards the kind of pot to use, clay or plastic pots are equally as good as each other. Once again it is left to the preference of the grower, although plastic pots are certainly easier to obtain these days. As to size of pot, African violets prefer to be slightly pot-bound at all stages of their growth and so the pot size is important. Plants should never be over-potted because excess compost causes the leaf and flower growth to slow down whilst the roots grow to fill the pot. Therefore always use the smallest pot possible for the size of the plant.

For mature plants, a good guide to pot size is that the pot diameter should be one third of the diameter across the foliage of a single-crowned plant. Because African violets are not deep rooted, it is better to grow them in dwarf or half pots. It is more difficult to decide on pot diameter when growing trailing hybrids, as nowadays wide, shallow pans are often used so that the branching stems may be pinned down for a better display. In this instance it is for the grower to decide on the size of pan for the plant so that it does not appear to be either over- or under-potted. If pinning down of the stems is not wanted, always consider the type size of the trailer and choose a size of dwarf or half pot that complements the plant.

Hanging baskets are currently very popular and may be used for the growing of trailing African violets, that are not intended for show, by planting several into and around a basket. However, hanging baskets tend to be too large for their ideal display, so a single plant in a hanging pot is a much better idea. These pots are available in sizes from 6in (15cm) in diameter as against 10in (25cm) diameter baskets. Also available are plastic hangers that may be attached to ordinary plastic pots of any size from 3in (7.5cm) diameter upwards, enabling small-sized plants to be displayed to advantage.

It is good practice to root-prune and repot any African violets that are not needed for exhibition at least once every twelve months; the best time of year is in the spring as the outdoor temperature begins to rise and light levels increase.

WATERING

There is no mystery about how to water, the mystery is in when to water, and there is no hard and fast rule as to exactly when a plant will need to be watered. It is useless to say 'Today is Tuesday, all the plants must be watered', because one plant might need watering while several others alongside do not. One learns when to water by experience, and by knowing the conditions in which the plants are growing. In fact more African violets die by drowning than by any other cause. As a rule of thumb, most of the rootball should be just moist at all times to allow the very fine root hairs to carry out their function of taking in water, air and nutrients. If the compost is either waterlogged or dried out, the root system cannot carry out its proper function so the plant will wilt and die. Thus to decide *when* a plant should be watered, use the finger tips to feel whether the compost is moist about half an inch (1cm) below its surface. If it feels dry there, water the plant; if in doubt, do not water but wait until the following day and test again. Moistness is difficult to describe: our definition is very damp, but not wet.

Some say that a plant should be left to wilt before watering it. In our experience this is not advisable, as by that time the tips of the root hairs will have been damaged, and flooding with water will cause all the roots to rot and the plant will die. If inadvertently a plant does dry out for a short period, water should be given in very small amounts over a period of two or three days to restore the compost to the correct moistness, thereby helping growth to continue.

There are several ways of watering a plant: onto the compost from the top; into the compost from the bottom of the pot; by standing the pot on capillary matting; by a wettable wick from a reservoir; by Texas style potting; and hydroponically.

Top Watering

The water is poured onto the compost without wetting the leaves. Enough water should be given for it to moisten the compost completely and then drain from the bottom of the pot; the surplus must be discarded. This is a preferred watering method for African violets being grown on window-sills. Any water falling on leaves and left there when the plant is in bright light or in a draught can damage them, and cause unsightly brown patches to develop. If water does fall onto the leaves it must be removed using a soft tissue.

Bottom Watering

Water is poured into the saucer or dish in which the plant is standing. More water should be added to the saucer if the plant soaks up all of the first amount in less than ten minutes. Any water remaining in the saucer or dish after twenty minutes should be discarded and the pot left to drain. This method is also suitable for window-sill growing of African violets. However, it is advisable periodically to water copiously from the top because excess harmful salts will have collected on the surface of the compost and this will flush them out. Care must be taken following this water flushing that thorough draining is allowed.

Capillary Matting

Plants standing on capillary matting will take up any water poured onto the matting provided there is good contact between the holes in the bottom of the pot and the matting surface. Care should be taken that the matting does not remain flooded for longer than forty-five minutes at a stretch. This method of watering has the added advantage of providing extra humidity for the plants, and is useful when several African violet plants are placed together on a window-sill tray.

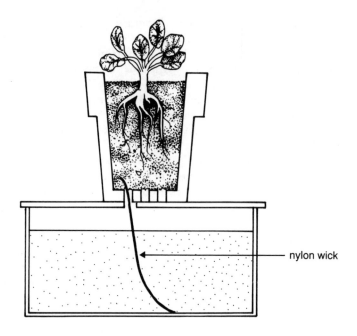

nylon wick

Wick watering.

Wettable Wick

Wick watering from a reservoir is very useful when African violets are left unattended for any lengthy period of time. A lidded container, such as a tub that you would normally throw away, is easily made into a reservoir. A hole should be cut in the centre of the lid for the wick to pass from the bottom of the pot into the water in the reservoir. A narrow wick, no more than half an inch (1cm) wide, cut from an old pair of nylon stockings or tights is best, and should be long enough to stretch from inside the pot to lie along the bottom of the reservoir. String, cotton or wool should not be used as these materials will rot if kept constantly wet, causing problems for the plants. The wick should be thoroughly wetted before one end is inserted into the compost at the bottom of the pot; capillary action will begin immediately the other end is placed in the water in the reservoir.

Texas Style Potting

This uses a pot with holes not only in the bottom but also around the side, about one third of the pot height above the base. For this method plastic pots must be used so that the side holes may be drilled out. The pot is

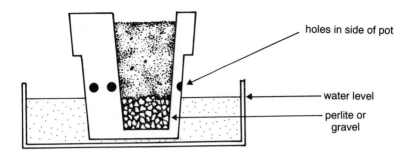

Texas style potting.

filled to the level of the holes in the side with gravel or perlite, and on top of this is placed a thin layer of compost; the plant is then potted in the normal manner. The potted plant stands constantly in a wide dish containing water, which is at a depth below the level of the holes in the side. Thus the compost is always kept moist, and air is allowed to circulate around the roots of the plant. However, although the pot is continually standing in water with this method, the compost will not become waterlogged. Texas style potting can be used as a constant feed method, and if so the pot should be flushed through with plain tepid water periodically.

Hydroponics

This is a method of growing plants without compost. Instead, hard-baked porous clay granules are used to support a plant upright in a waterproof container and the growing medium is actually a solution of a fertilizer in water. In order for the plant to increase in growth its roots need to absorb not only liquid – the fertilizer solution – but also air. The ability to do this is owed to the roots being of a different type to those that grow in compost. Water roots do not have root hairs: they are thicker walled and have larger channels within them for the transfer of liquid and gas through to the rest of the plant.

The usual procedure in hydroponics is for all the roots initially to be submerged in liquid; as this is absorbed its level in the container of granules is reduced and many of the roots are left surrounded by air. Care must be taken that the granules do not dry out completely, thus damaging the roots; inclusion of a liquid level indicator prevents this happening. In some hydroponic containers available commercially, a float is incorporated; this is graduated to show the liquid level so the grower knows when to replenish the fertilizer solution. In fact it is not necessary to buy such a system; something similar could be made up as long as some kind of liquid level indicator is used.

The fertilizers given to hydroponically grown plants are usually of a different formulation to those for compost-grown plants. However, we see no reason why the latter cannot be used provided they are diluted greatly. The dilution factor would have to be determined by experiment and assessment of the performance of the plant.

Not only do the granules support the plant in an upright position, but being porous they also absorb the fertilizer solution; as the liquid level reduces in the container they will release that which is absorbed to the roots, which are clinging to it and growing into individual granules. With a good root system it is possible to lift the entire rootball of granules out of the container in the same way as when a plant is grown in compost.

It is possible to transfer a compost-grown African violet to hydroponic growing fairly easily because compost roots are capable of changing to water roots; water roots, on the other hand, are not capable of becoming compost roots. In selecting a waterproof container for potting up a plant, a larger size is required than would normally be used for potting into compost due to the granules not packing as closely as compost. The African violet to be transferred should either have all the compost washed off the roots or most of the compost carefully shaken off its rootball before being bedded into the porous clay granules. Enough fertilizer solution should be added to the container barely to cover the granules initially, and this level will reduce a little as the granules absorb it. It may be necessary to give the transferred African violet extra humidity until it establishes itself to the new growing method. This could be achieved by enclosing it in a large polythene bag for a week or two.

Hydroponic growing has its advantages in that the grower is able to assess easily from the level indicator when more fertilizer solution needs to be added, and also in that re-potting is required less frequently because the root system produced by the plant is smaller. If an African violet plantlet is to be grown on by this method, we think that a fertilizer for foliage plants should be used, as with a compost-grown plantlet, until a mature size has been achieved and then one for flowering plants should be used.

The technique of growing hydroponically is so entirely different from compost growing that it should be tried only on expendable plants until sufficient experience has been gained; only then transfer more of the collection to the method.

Within the past year a method for growing plants hydroponically has come onto the market in the UK under the label of 'Seramis'. The packs of hard-baked but very porous clay granules are to be found in garden centres together with water indicators that are inserted into the rootball of the plant. When fertilizer solution needs to be added to the waterproof plant container, the indicator changes in colour from blue to red. Also available are the special fertilizers needed for growing by this method, one for flowering plants and

Saintpaulia shumensis: *miniature species used in breeding modern miniature and semi-miniature hybrids.*

Saintpaulia velutina: *discovered in the West Usambara Mountains in 1916.*

Saintpaulia ionantha: *the first identified species.*

'Frosted Whisper'. Single, ruffled, star; quilted 'Tommie Lou' variegate; large. (Scott, USA)

'Skagit's Ambassador'. Single, bicoloured, ruffled; large. (Lindstrom, USA)

'China Pink'. Semi-double, ruffled, star; tailored; standard. (Fredette, USA)

'Colonial Canberra'. Semi-double, frilled, multicoloured; tailored; standard. (Ham, Australia)

'Chiffon Vesper'. Single to semi-double, bicoloured, star; tailored; standard. (Hill, UK)

'Mauna Loa'. Single, chimera; tailored; standard. (Eyerdom, USA)

'Garnet Halo'. Semi-double to double; tailored, 'Tommie Lou' variegate, red-backed; large. (Boone, USA)

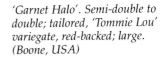

'Suncoast Seabreeze'. Double, ruffled, bordered multicolour; wavy; standard. (Williams, USA)

'Windy Day'. Semi-double, fringed, star; ruffled; standard. (Boone, USA)

The first yellow hybrid, displayed at the African Violet Society of America's Convention in 1990. (Blansit, USA)

'Tiger'. Semi-double; tailored, variegate; large. (Fredette, USA)

Glenedd Saintpaulias. Display at Chelsea Flower Show 1994.

'Red Mount Fuji'. Single, chimera. Colour mutation from Japan.

'Maggie May'. Double, geneva; tailored; standard. (African Violet Centre, UK)

'Majesty'. Double, frilled, multicoloured (with yellow); wavy, serrated; standard. (Blansit, USA)

'Playful Dreamer'. Semi-double, wavy, multicoloured (with yellow); tailored; standard. (Sorano/Blansit, USA)

'Silver Milestone'. Single to semi-double, geneva; quilted; standard. (Hill, UK) Named for the Silver Jubilee of the Saintpaulia and Houseplant Society.

'Dancin' Trail'. Double, star; pointed, red-backed; semi-miniature trailer. (Sorano, USA)

'Tomahawk'. Semi-double to double; tailored; large. (Stork, USA)

'Centenary'. Double, geneva; quilted; standard. (African Violet Centre, UK)

one for foliage plants. It is understood that plants may be propagated from cuttings by the Seramis method; at present we are experimenting with this, and so do not wish to give set advice until we have had more experience. However, we see no reason why the reader should not try using Seramis now, and learn a different way of growing African violets.

The Water

No matter which watering method is used, it is most important that the water itself should be either at room temperature or tepid when used, and at a suitable pH value. Water supplied by the various water companies can differ widely in its pH value, so check with your local company; they will give the information you need. Water of a high alkalinity, for example pH 7.5 and above, may be treated in the home in various ways to make it acceptable to African violets. It may be boiled and left to cool before using, or as previously stated, one teaspoon (5ml) of distilled white vinegar may be added per gallon (4.5 litres) of water. With extreme alkalinity it will be necessary to use water that has been through a horticultural softening filter. This does *not* mean a water softener fitted into a domestic water supply, as this type replaces the hardness causing alkalinity with sodium salts and these are poisonous to plants.

Rainwater is good for African violets, provided that when taken from the waterbutt it is filtered to remove any bits and pieces present, then boiled to kill bugs and bacteria, and cooled before use.

RELATIVE HUMIDITY

There is another important factor associated with watering, and that is to maintain a state of humidity around the plants. Invisible water vapour produces a relative humidity, and this creates a beneficial micro-climate for African violets whereby transpiration of moisture from their leaves is lessened and the appearance of flowers and foliage is greatly enhanced. A relative humidity between 50 and 70 per cent would be advantageous, whereas below 40 per cent is too low – this will cause flowers to be sparse and small, whilst buds will go brown and drop; also the leaves will lack their normal lustre, their tips becoming brown in the low humidity. Small relative humidity meters are available from garden centres and may be placed adjacent to the plants to give the relevant readings.

Ways to Increase Relative Humidity

In living room conditions, low relative humidity is the norm and it must be rectified for plants to thrive. This may be done by grouping plants, standing them over water or on capillary matting, and by misting.

Grouping Plants Placing several plants together is a simple way of slightly increasing relative humidity. Each plant will help its neighbours by producing a micro-climate, and thus even less water vapour will be lost by each plant so the stomata on the leaves will close. In hot weather, however, and when central heating is needed, grouping plants does not produce a large enough increase in the humidity. A slightly higher level can be created by standing the grouped plants in bowls of moist peat; although it must be remembered to lift the plants out of the peat periodically so that their roots are prevented from growing into it.

Standing over Water Another method used to increase humidity is to stand the plants on constantly wet gravel held in trays. Care must be taken that the plant pots are not standing in the water: the rule is *above* the water, not in it. The water in the tray should be changed frequently, and the tray and gravel washed so that they do not become encrusted with limescale and any small particles of compost falling from the pots.

Capillary Matting Window-sill trays holding plants may also be lined with capillary matting; this should be kept constantly moist but not wet to produce extra humidity for the plants. Again, the matting should be washed frequently to remove the excess salts left after the evaporation of water from the matting. Good contact between the pot base and matting usually means that some fine particles of compost soak into the matting, and these should also be washed out.

Misting In very hot conditions, plants may be misted twice a day using a sprayer: this should contain hand-hot but not boiling water, and it should be held about 2ft (60cm) away from and above the plants so that a fog falls on them. The sprayer action which causes the formation of miniscule droplets drastically cools the temperature of the water; this means that if the water used in the sprayer is cooler than hand hot the mist or fog falling onto the plants would be icy cold. In this event the plants would be severely chilled and brown patches on the leaves would result. Any excess moisture settled on the leaves or in the centre crown must be removed using a soft tissue, and the plants allowed to dry out of draughts or direct sunlight.

The difference between misting and spraying should be appreciated. The difference is in the size of the droplets falling onto the plants. In spraying the droplets are much larger than in misting due to the sprayer being held nearer to the plants.

FEEDING

Sometimes the importance of feeding an indoor plant is overlooked by many people, who seem to think that a plant will grow without any help from them; they are then disappointed when it withers away and dies. It is important to understand what each nutritional element of a fertilizer will do, the major elements being nitrogen (N), phosphorus (P) and potassium (K).

Nitrogen

This element has an essential effect on foliage growth because it helps to build the green chlorophyll; thus it is greatly involved in the production of sugars for use by the plant. Shortage of nitrogen results in leaves turning yellow, and so a plant ceases to thrive. Too much nitrogen makes for an abundance of leaf growth to the detriment of flower production.

Phosphorus

This element is almost as important as nitrogen in that it is involved in converting plant starch into sugar; thus it promotes good flowering and strong stems and roots. To show how effective it is in promoting flowering, a mature plant that is reluctant to flower may be boosted into bud initiation by giving it a small amount of superphosphate. Enough to cover a one penny piece thinly is sprinkled over the compost surface and watered in. This dose is repeated two weeks later, and it is usual that within six weeks of the initial dose of superphosphate buds will be just showing.

Potassium

The main effect of potassium is on the root system, helping it to absorb other nutrients and promoting vigour in the plant. It is also said to make plants more resistant to disease and to cause them to withstand cooler temperatures.

Trace Elements

Other elements in very small amounts also need to be present in a fertilizer, and they are listed on the label as trace elements. These include iron, magnesium, manganese, boron, copper, zinc and vitamins, and all these help to make a plant sturdy and healthy. It is normal for all commercial fertilizers sold for houseplants to include all the trace elements. When pH values in the compost are above 7.0, many of these trace elements are locked in and cannot be absorbed by the root system – another pointer to the importance of ensuring the correct pH value in growing plants.

Which Fertilizer?

The foregoing shows that when buying a fertilizer for plants it is important to decide what it is needed for and then to observe the NPK formula. Thus, young plants need to grow foliage to reach maturity and so a fertilizer with a higher content of nitrogen is required; but once mature, a plant will want to begin to flower, and so one must look for higher contents of phosphorus and potassium than of nitrogen in a fertilizer. An example of a high nitrogen fertilizer is one sold for use on green foliage houseplants with an NPK formula such as 6:2:2; whilst one with a low nitrogen formulation has NPK figures such as 12:36:14. A balanced fertilizer has an NPK formula of 20:20:20 and may be used as an all-round feed for plants.

There are so many proprietary fertilizers on the market, and all have slightly different formulations of NPK; but even so, they all fall within the description of being either high, low or balanced in nitrogen. There are also organic feeds containing fish emulsion: these are high in nitrogen and are good for use on young plants, but they can have a strong odour even when used at a very weak dilution. The choice of make is for the grower to decide. However, it sometimes helps the African violets if two different fertilizers of the same type are alternated occasionally; a change of food is good for everything.

Over the years the authors have found that it is beneficial to their plants to use a fertilizer at a more diluted strength, and more frequently than is recommended by the manufacturer. Following this maxim of little and often the amount of dilution, and how often this dilute feed is given, depends upon the method of watering. For top and bottom watering, a dilution to one quarter the recommended strength given at every watering may be used, whilst for wick watering and Texas style potting the reservoir and dish are filled with a one-eighth strength solution. These latter methods are termed 'constant feeding'. However, it is not advisable to pour fertilizer solution onto capillary matting to feed plants, because as the water in the solution evaporates from the matting, the solution becomes too concentrated; and too strong a fertilizer solution is detrimental to the growth of the plants because it retards the development of young leaves in the growing crown. A symptom of this is seen in the formation of minute brown crystals on young leaf margins, caused by the exudation of excess salts.

No matter which method of feeding a plant is used, there is always a build-up of salts in the top layer of compost due to evaporation of water vapour. If these salts are left for a long period of time, the African violet main stem will be affected, to the extent of rotting. An unsightly white crust is also formed around the rim of the pot, and this can cause a leaf stalk to be scarred and to rot where it touches the pot rim. To prevent either of these problems occurring, the compost should be flushed through with copious amounts of plain, tepid water once every six weeks to wash away these excess salts, and afterwards the plant should be allowed to drain for about half an hour before being returned to its original position.

For very young plants and those still on their mother leaf, a foliar feed is beneficial as the leaves are able to take up fertilizer more easily than the roots at these stages of growth. A foliar fertilizer may also be used to feed a plant whose roots have been a little damaged, although normally it is not a substitute for root feeding. Only a specific foliar fertilizer, which usually has equal percentages of N and P with a slightly lower percentage of K, should be used in this way. To avoid unsightly marking of the African violet leaves by the feed, spray every four to five days for four to six weeks with a dilution using hand-hot water to one quarter the recommended strength, applied from a sprayer held about 2ft (60cm) away from the plants. Any large droplets falling or collecting in the centre of the growing crown should be removed with a soft tissue, and the plants allowed to dry in a warm atmosphere out of bright light.

It is best not to be tempted to make up feed for plants at a strength greater than the recommended dilution on the manufacturer's label, as this will definitely damage the delicate leaves of the centre crown.

VARIEGATED FOLIAGE HYBRIDS

There may be times when there are difficulties in bringing variegated foliage African violets to peak condition. Although their cultivation follows that of green foliage hybrids fairly closely, there are a few differences. They are slower growing because they have less chlorophyll in their leaves, and they are also slower to flower. To keep their variegation they should be fed with a very low nitrogen fertilizer, having a formula such as NPK 0:10:10 or 5:50:17. However, if a plant loses the green in its leaves, so becoming mainly white or cream, it should then be fed with a high nitrogen fertilizer and placed in a warmer position for about four weeks or until normal variegation returns. Greening will also be encouraged if a weak solution of Epsom salts (magnesium sulphate) is given to the plants once a week for about four weeks. During periods of hot weather, African violets with crown or mosaic types of variegation may become all-green leaved. In this instance the normal variegation will return in the new leaves once the weather cools. 'Tommie Lou' variegation does not appear to have this problem.

GROWING IN THE GREENHOUSE

The average hobby greenhouse would have to be specially equipped for African violets to be grown in it successfully, and in fact the conditions required for them would mean that little other than certain plants requiring very similar conditions could be grown alongside.

The average greenhouse is very difficult to keep cool enough in the summer months unless it is heavily shaded, very well ventilated, and equipped with electric fans to give gentle air circulation rather than a strong blast of air; lighting under the benches is also necessary to utilize those areas. In winter, with the shading removed, the greenhouse would have to have very good insulation, and electric rather than oil or gas heating to maintain a minimum temperature of 60°F (15°C) as well as fans to keep the air gently moving (oil and gas heating is notorious for producing fumes and excessive water vapour, which would not suit African violets at the lower temperatures). Extra lighting to extend the natural day-length would have to be fitted, in addition to that already under the benches; moreover both systems would require separate time switches so that both areas had the same total hours of light. Benching would have to be strong enough to support the weight of wet sand or gravel for the plants to stand upon, and care would have to be taken to ensure that no water on the top of the bench could come into contact with the lighting equipment below it. A further disadvantage is that infestation by a variety of insects and infection by diseases can very easily invade a greenhouse at any time.

In our opinion it would have to be a very enthusiastic grower to go to these lengths to grow African violets in a greenhouse. Certainly the commercial growers have problems even when fully equipped. It would be much easier and cheaper to convert a room in a house into a plant room, and much more enjoyable.

5

PROPAGATION

It is inherent in the human character that when people like a plant they feel compelled to propagate it to get more, and the easier this is to do, the more likely it is to be done. There is no doubt that it is easy to propagate African violets, especially as there are several methods to increase successfully the number of plants from one. These methods are from a leaf, by a sucker or offset, by division and by seed.

PROPAGATING FROM A LEAF

All but one type of African violet propagate easily from leaves, although for greatest success the correct leaf must be selected. Thus the leaf must be mature and still have a good deal of potential growth in it; it is a mistake to take an old, nearly spent leaf from the outermost layer of leaves, because although it will produce plantlets it will take a long time to do so and they will not grow into such good mature plants. Nor should a young leaf from the centre of the crown be taken, as leaves do not achieve their full potential for propagation until they have grown to full size. Also its removal from the crown will spoil the shape of the plant. For rosette

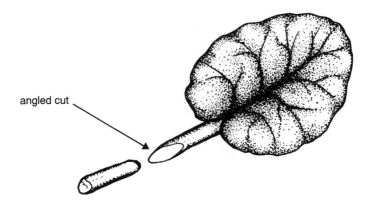

angled cut

Leaf trimmed ready for potting.

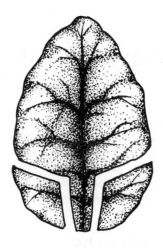

Leaf without a stalk trimmed to make a stalk.

hybrid
name label

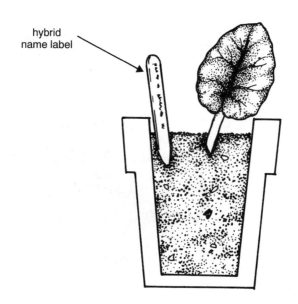

Leaf potted into compost.

types, a leaf from the second or third layer of leaves from the outside would be the most appropriate. With trailing hybrids, a leaf from a similar layer on one of the branches should be removed for propagation.

The leaf is taken cleanly from the main stem of a rosette or the branch stem of a trailer by a sharp sideways tug so that no stub remains, as this could rot and infect the main stem. If a stub is left it should be removed as closely as possible to the stem. The leaf petiole should be trimmed to a length of 1.5in (4cm) and cleanly cut at a slanting angle using a sharp-bladed knife or razor blade. The slanting cut is to expose a large area of tissue from which roots and plantlets will grow.

Sometimes one is given a leaf of a choice or rare hybrid, and its petiole is accidently broken off at the base of the leaf blade. All is not lost, however, because a short stalk can be made by cutting away a small section of the leaf blade on either side of the main vein. This cut leaf may then be propagated following the normal method.

When propagating variegated hybrids, the leaf taken should have as much green colour in it as possible. Even an all-green leaf from a variegate will produce variegated plantlets.

Rooting in Compost
A leaf from a standard or large-sized plant should be potted one to a 2in (5cm) pot so that the minimum amount of moist compost may be used. With smaller sized plants it is best to pot two leaves back-to-back in a 2in (5cm) pot. The reason for this is so that roots can quickly fill the pot, thus allowing the plantlets to grow quickly. The pot should then be labelled with the name of the hybrid and the date of potting.

Some hybrids have very large leaves, and these would easily fall over if potted into small pots. These large leaves may be potted into a polystyrene cup that has had one side cut away to half its depth so that the leaf blade may be supported at its back by the remaining rim of the cup. We have found it unnecessary to use hormone rooting powder, as African violet leaves root quickly providing the correct one has been taken. The potted leaf should be put into a covered propagator or enclosed in a polythene bag, and placed in a warm, brightly lit position out of direct sunlight. If condensation builds up on the inside of the polythene bag it should be opened to allow the excess moisture to escape, and then closed again. Leaves will root just as easily when potted into small pots of moist vermiculite.

Rooting in Water
African violet leaves may also be rooted in water using a dark-coloured container such as a tablet bottle or a film cassette box of an appropriate size. Clear containers should be avoided, as the cut end of a leaf petiole will curl towards the brightest side of such a container. A small square of

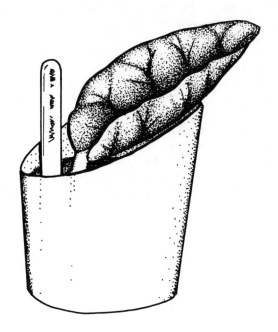

Large-size leaf potted into a styrene cup.

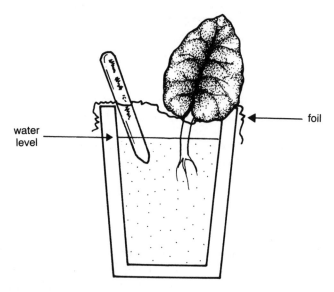

water
level

foil

Leaf rooting in water.

aluminium foil is secured over the top of the container after it is about three quarters filled with water. The trimmed base of the petiole is pushed thorugh a central hole in the foil, and should be positioned so it is barely touching the water; it is therefore essential to top up the water level if evaporation occurs. It is not advisable to allow roots to grow longer than 0.5in (1cm) before potting the leaf into a small pot of compost, as longer roots are water roots and do not convert easily to compost roots. Leaves with water roots when potted into compst do not proceed quickly to plantlet production, in fact not until compost roots have grown; so the time spent producing those long water roots has in effect been wasted.

Although not advisable, it is possible to allow long water roots to grow and plantlets to develop in the water. In this instance the leaf with its plantlets should be potted into moist compost and then allowed to grow very much larger before separation.

Growing on
Roots should have grown in six to eight weeks, and you can test if they have because then you will be able to lift the pot, leaf and compost all together by holding just the leaf tip in one's fingers. Plantlets should be starting to

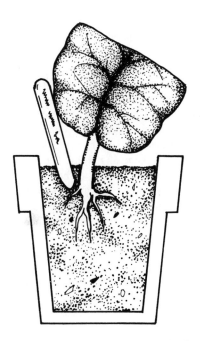

Top half of large rooted leaf broken away to encourage plantlet production.

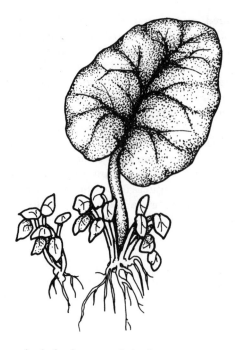

Plantlets on mother leaf and a separated plantlet.

show above the compost in a further six to eight weeks, though this will depend upon the hybrid as some produce quickly whilst others can be very slow. At times a leaf is reluctant to put up plantlets and will itself grow larger; this sort may be encouraged to produce them by breaking off the upper half of its blade. The number of plantlets that a leaf produces can sometimes be amazing. On average the number is around four or five, although sometimes a leaf will produce only one, but there are hybrids that are extremely prolific, producing up to twenty and at times more. When this happens the heart must be hardened into discarding a percentage of them and potting up only the sturdiest. The wonder is that even after producing such a number the leaf can be retrimmed, potted, and will produce plantlets once again that are just as numerous and sturdy as the first crop.

When plantlets can be seen, and when watering is necessary, feeding should begin with a very weak dilution – say, at one-tenth strength – of a high nitrogen fertilizer such as fish emulsion. As the plantlets grow they should be hardened off by gradually removing the propagator top or opening the polythene bag daily for an hour or two, and be given a weak foliar feed. When they are 1.5 to 2in (4 to 5cm) tall and each have a minimum of four leaves, they are ready to be separated from their mother leaf and potted individually into 2in (5cm) pots, with the exception of variegated hybrids.

The variegates quite often produce plantlets with very little green in their leaves, and should be left on the mother leaf until they become much more green. If separated too soon they will not be capable of survival as they are dependent upon their mother leaf for sustenance. Greening up of these plantlets will be encouraged by giving several weak feeds of fish emulsion or any high nitrogen fertilizer, and by keeping them in warmer and lighter conditions.

The potted plantlets should be stood in a tray lined with capillary matting that has been thoroughly wetted and then wrung out. Initially they are given a weak foliar feed to settle them into their new environment, and after about three weeks the feeding programme is changed to alternating a high nitrogen and a high phosphate fertilizer at one-eighth strength for every watering, with an occasional watering of plain tepid water.

When the roots of young standard or large-sized African violets have filled their pots, they are potted on into 2.5in (7cm) pots, given another foliar feed, then three weeks later the same feeding programme is followed as previously, using high nitrogen and high phosphate fertilizers. They may be left in this size pot until budding is initiated, when they should be potted on into 3.5in (9cm) pots. With miniature and semi-miniature plants it is advisable not to pot on in the first instance but to repot into a clean pot of the same size, gently teasing away a little of the compost at the bottom of the rootball so that a small amount of fresh compost may be added. The same feeding programme should be followed as for the larger sized plants. The maximum size of pot for miniature and semi-miniature rosette hybrids is 2.5in (7cm) even when mature.

Trailing hybrids should have the same treatment as described above, but if by the time the standard and large-sized trailers are potted into 3 or 3.5in (8 or 9cm) pots they have not begun to branch, the growing tip should be carefully and cleanly cut out. A similar procedure should be followed with the miniature and semi-miniature trailing hybrids, except that the pot size is 2.5in (7cm). This cutting out of the tip will encourage branching from the lower leaf axils.

Odd Happenings Do not be surprised to see a flower stalk grow from a young plantlet whilst it is still on its mother leaf. It may seem odd, but it happens sometimes and is not in the least detrimental. At the very least it will give early intimation as to whether or not the plantlet is likely to be true to the catalogue description of the flower, although frequently the first flowers of a semi-double flowered hybrid will be single.

Although the following happens infrequently from vegetative propagation, a plantlet may be produced that does not have the appearance of its

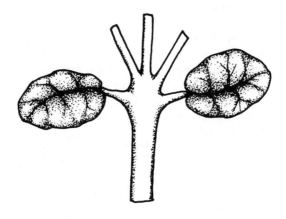

Chimera flower stalk trimmed for potting.

parent or siblings in some way, either in leaf form or flower colour and form. This is a *mutant* or *sport* and should be labelled as such. Further leaf propagation of this mutant should be carried out to ascertain whether or not it is stable, and if it proves to be so, then it should be labelled as 'Sport of . . .' and not given a new name.

Chimeras

This type of African violet poses a slight problem in its propagation because it does not come true to pattern by the normal leaf method. Plants grown from their leaves will rarely have flowers with the pinwheel pattern, but are more likely to have flowers of a solid colour. To explain, chimera African violets have two genetically different tissues side by side, an outer and an inner layer in the petioles. Normally roots and plantlets grow from the inner tissue layer, therefore the original chimera is not produced because the outer tissue layer, which must be in the make-up of the propagated plant, is not in the plantlet.

There are certain leaves which may be used for propagation, namely the usually insignificant two small leaves behind the inflorescence on the flower peduncle. Flowers above these leaves should be removed so that very short pedicel stubs remain – but without damaging the base of the stubs – and the peduncle cut through about 0.75in (2cm) below the tiny leaves. This cutting is inserted into a small pot of moist compost or vermiculite so that the leaf axils are level with the surface of the compost; it is then treated as a normal leaf cutting. Minute plantlets will grow from the axils of the two tiny leaves, and when large enough they should be potted up individually and grown on as any other plantlet.

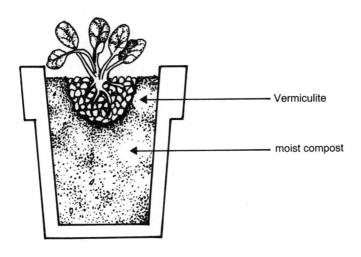

Sucker potted into pocket of vermiculate to encourage early rooting.

PROPAGATING FROM A SUCKER OR OFFSET

Sometimes a rosette type of African violet will produce a tiny sucker or offset in a leaf axil instead of a flower stalk. If allowed to continue to grow in this position, suckers will cause a plant to become multi-crowned and so mis-shapen as to be useless for exhibition purposes. However, if the sucker is carefully eased away from the leaf axil when it has six to eight leaves, it may be used to grow into another plant. Care must be taken that no damage, or very little, is done to its rounded base when removing it.

A small pot is filled with moist compost, and a small hole made in the centre surface; this is filled with damp vermiculite into which the sucker base is inserted. As the vermiculite is sterile and without any food value, roots grow quickly and spread into the surrounding compost. The sucker should then be kept in a humid, warm and light position out of direct sunlight, and grown on as a plantlet.

The quickest way to propagate a trailing African violet to get a good-looking plant is by cutting off a short branch – which is actually an elongated sucker – just above a leaf node and rooting it down in a pot of compost and vermiculite as for a sucker. Because the base of the cutting is a stem without leaves, it is much less likely to suffer problems in rooting. Taking this cutting is also useful to the original plant, as its stem will then branch again.

The usual way of propagating chimera African violets so as to keep the true flower pinwheel pattern is by sucker growth. Plants can be induced to produce suckers from leaf axils either by carefully removing just the centre growing point, or by beheading the plant. The latter method gives a new plant quickly by being rooted down, and later suckers to increase the number. It needs some courage for a fairly new grower to behead a plant, but it is very worthwhile if chimeras need to be propagated. A word of warning, however: extra care must be taken that the base of a chimera sucker is not damaged in any way. A nice rounded sucker base can be obtained if you remove the leaf below it early on, thus allowing the sucker to spread out; then when it is of good size, a gentle sideways tug will take it cleanly away from the main stem of the old plant. Don't be too greedy: don't allow more than two suckers to grow on an old plant at a time; they will then be much better quality for growing on. When they are removed, others will probably grow from other leaf axils, and the old plant will not be so stressed as to stop growing.

PROPAGATING FROM SEED

African violet seed is dust-fine and requires very careful handling before being sown – one sneeze or cough and you have lost it all! The method that we have found to give the most successful results is as follows:

A small shallow pan such as a margarine tub, with drainage holes made in the bottom and a layer of perlite in it about 0.5in (1cm) deep, is filled with fine moist compost. It is stood in a dish of warm water until the compost surface is seen to be thoroughly wet, when it is removed and allowed to drain for at least two hours. The seed is sown very thinly onto the compost; it should *not* be covered with more compost *nor* with fine vermiculite. Like all gesneriads, African violet seed needs light to germinate. The pan should be covered with clear plastic film to create a humid atmosphere for the seed, and either kept in a warm, light position out of direct sunlight, or placed under fluorescent lights. Alternatively, the uncovered pan may be placed in a heated, covered propagator running at 70°F (21°C). When the first sign of germination is apparent in three weeks or less, the pan should be taken from the propagator, covered with clear plastic film and placed on a window-sill out of direct sunlight or under fluorescent lights.

Do not start worrying if germination takes longer than three weeks. The time it takes can depend upon how fresh the seed is, although it has been known for seed as old as four years to germinate in six to eight weeks. But sometimes apparently fresh seed does not germinate because it is not viable. Always leave a seed pan for several months before giving up on the seed and discarding it.

As the seedlings grow, great care must be taken that the compost does not dry out; watering involves standing the pan in a dish holding 0.5in (1cm) of tepid water for ten to fifteen minutes to allow the perlite in the bottom of the pan to soak up the water. Once the seedlings have four tiny leaves they may be pricked out into quarter-size seed trays of moist compost, and covered with clear plastic film. The exception to this is with the all-white seedlings growing from seed of variegates: it is pointless to prick these out because they will not grow any more as they lack chlorophyll. However, all-green seedlings, or those with only a little green in their leaves, will grow on to be variegates and should be pricked out. When necessary water should be given from the bottom by standing the seedlings in a dish, and a quarter-strength high nitrogen fertilizer should be given at every other watering.

Once the seedlings are established and have grown so they touch the plastic film, this should be removed gradually to harden them off. As they grow on and their leaves begin to touch each other, the time has come to transplant them into individual small pots – these should be of a suitable size, in particular so they are not over-potted and do not have too much compost for their roots. Keep them in a warm, humid atmosphere for a few days so that they can recover from the transplanting. The seedlings should now be fed with an eighth-strength balanced fertilizer at every watering and grown on to maturity. Long before this the all-green seedlings of variegates will be showing their full variegation potential.

MICRO-PROPAGATION

Micro-propagation, or tissue culture, is a method used by commercial nurseries to produce very many plants of a hybrid in a comparatively short period of time. It is carried out in laboratories equipped with special facilities for controlled sterile conditions. It is not a propagation method that the average hobby grower at home is normally able to use.

The process entails a small section of an African violet leaf being cleaned and sterilized with chemicals, and then placed on an agar gel in a jar with a screw-down lid. The agar contains hormones and nutrients to induce shoot production, and within a week or two the leaf section will be covered with a multitude of shoots; it is then removed from the jar, divided and replaced in more sterile jars containing the same formula agar. Division continues until the number of shoots, which at this time do not have roots, is considered adequate for the required plant production. At this point all the shoots are transferred to sterile jars containing agar of a different formulation, this having hormones and nutrients that will promote root growth, and the shoots begin to grow roots. Sometimes roots have been known not to connect with a shoot, thus making the shoot useless. After about two months the agar is covered with a mass of minute plantlets which may then be teased apart into individual ones, pricked out into compost, and grown on into young plants under nursery conditions.

Although this method is advantageous to commercial nurseries in that very large numbers of plants are produced for sale, it has, in the authors' considered opinion, the disadvantage of producing a fair percentage of mutants and sports of the hybrid. This results in collectors being disappointed when, having purchased a young non-flowering plant of a named hybrid, it does not flower truly to the original description of that hybrid.

6

REJUVENATION OF OLD PLANTS

Many a time we have been shown a sad-looking old African violet that has two or three crowns, or that is overcrowded with crowns or has the beginnings of a neck or, worst of all, has a tuft of leaves on the top of a gnarled and twisted stem. The question then asked is what, if anything, can possibly be done to return it to some semblance of its early glory of flowering. Success may be achieved by division, root pruning and repotting, or decapitation.

DIVISION

It is easy to deal with an African violet that has two or three separate crowns that are actually separate plants. This sort of growth is usually the result of potting up the whole clump of plantlets produced by a leaf during propagation without separating them. When the plant is removed from its pot, as much as possible of the compost should be gently shaken away from the roots and each crown teased apart. Each crown should then be potted into the smallest possible sized pot with fresh moist compost. Preservation of humidity is not absolutely necessary in this case as the plants already have roots; however, standing the pots over a little water would be a good idea as the compost should be kept very slightly drier than normal for about one week in order that the roots have time to recover from the trauma of the plants being teased apart. In this instance the leaves would help recovery by closing their stomata to stop transpiration of water vapour for a day or so.

In the case of a plant which has been allowed to sucker from leaf axils for a long time and is overcrowded with crowns, more drastic means have to be employed. This multi-crowned plant will be very mis-shapen, flowering is more than likely to be sparse, and in all probability the plant will never have been repotted by its owner. Nevertheless, providing that in all other respects the plant is healthy, it would be worth dividing it into separate sucker crowns for rooting.

Firstly, the plant should be removed from its pot for ease of handling and the outer layer of old leaves should be taken off to expose some of the

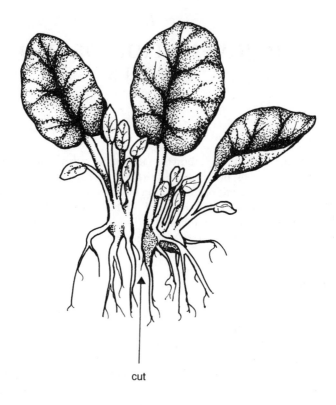

cut

Division of multi-crowned plant.

leaf axils where suckers are growing. These fairly large suckers may be carefully removed from the main stem by a gentle tug sideways at each rounded base; the smaller suckers may be cleanly cut away from the stem using a sharp small-bladed knife. As little damage as possible should be done to the sucker base, although any damage inflicted would not be unduly serious unless the plant was a chimera. It may be that more leaves have to be removed to expose all but the tiniest of suckers, and these are easily taken off with the point of a soft-leaded pencil; pencil is used because it leaves a smear of carbon which seals the tiny wound, thus preventing rot setting in. All suckers of a reasonable size should be potted up into small pots to develop roots and grow on (*see* page 75). Hopefully a suckerless crown of good size would remain, to be dealt with as a necked plant.

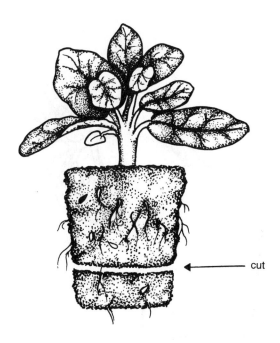

Rootball cut for re-potting of plant. Neck formed by removal of old leaves.

ROOT PRUNING AND REPOTTING

Any plant that has had a number of outer leaves removed should be root pruned and repotted. Repotting is not the same as potting on. A repotted plant is one that has been root pruned and then potted into a clean pot of the same size with a little fresh compost, whereas potting on is a plant being potted into a pot of one size larger than the original pot. The procedure entails firstly removing the plant from its pot and scraping away any old brown scar tissue at the bottom of the stem. Then the oldest portion of the rootball, that is the lowest one third to a half part, is cut away so that the exposed neck of the stem may be lowered into the clean pot. A little fresh moist compost is put into the clean pot and the remaining rootball is placed on top, with more fresh moist compost being filled in around the exposed neck from where new roots will grow. Care should be taken with watering for a week or two, so that the new roots are not growing into over-wet compost as this might cause their tips to rot.

Normally a mature plant should be repotted at least once a year when the removal of old leaves begins to expose a necked stem. Old leaves become pale and discoloured and are no help at all with plant growth, so

cut

Long-necked plant cut for trimming stem.

there is no point in keeping them on a plant. By repotting, a mature African violet may continue to grow well in the same size pot for many years. This is especially useful where many plants are grown on window-sills, when it is desirable for them to be kept at a sensible size for this purpose. It has been known for an African violet that has been repotted annually to be still as beautiful as it was more than twenty years before.

DECAPITATION

A plant that has never been repotted and has a long leafless stem with a tuft of leaves on its top is termed 'long necked'. Often the stem looks gnarled with leaf scars, and is twisted and bent over the rim of its pot. In this state the ordinary repotting that has been described is useless, and what amounts to major decapitation surgery is desperately needed by the plant – and requiring good nerves on the part of the owner.

The stem should be completely cut through with a sharp-bladed knife 0.75in (2cm) below the tuft of leaves, and any leaves in excess of eight should be taken off. The corky tissue covering old leaf scars should be

Crown of long-necked plant trimmed ready for potting.

gently scraped away from the stem, and the base of the latter trimmed into a cone shape. The plant crown thus formed is set into vermiculite and compost as for a sucker (*see* page 75) covered to preserve humidity for the remaining leaves, and kept in a warm position out of direct sunlight until rooted. The new plant should be weaned gradually to a lower humidity, and continued to be grown on to maturity and flowering.

It is also possible to root such a crown in water by the method used for rooting leaves in water. However, in this instance it is important that the crown is potted into compost by the time the new roots are 0.5in (1cm) long so that water roots are not grown.

The reader may not believe that the severed main stem can be kept growing in its original pot to produce suckers from leaf scars just below the cut. The old scar tissue should not be removed as this would prevent the initiation of a sucker from that point. Until tiny suckers are apparent the rootball should be kept somewhat drier than normal, but not completely dry because the roots need to be kept alive. Without leaves on the main stem to transpire, the rootball will remain moist for a longer time, but nonetheless frequent attention to the plant's moistness is needed. When the suckers are well grown, with a crown of at least six leaves, they may be carefully removed from the old stem and potted up for rooting. Growing suckers from an old stem is not really necessary, but it is interesting to do just to prove it can be done and to gain more experience of what a wonderful plant an African violet can be.

When lecturing on African violets the authors usually include a demonstration of the decapitation surgery and root pruning, and always hear gasps of horror from their audiences at these rejuvenation practices. Be assured the procedures are successful and easy to carry out: all that is needed is a little courage, the know-how, and a sharp-bladed knife.

7

HYBRIDIZATION

As soon as success with propagation has been achieved, the thoughts of a grower almost invariably turn to hybridizing an entirely new African violet from seed. Of course, the very first plants that are grown from seed of one's own crossing are the world's best, no matter what the parents and it is only later, with experience, that you recognize that those seedlings regarded with so much pride were probably not worth the growing, when you realize that a little about genetics as well as the background of the parent plants must be known to produce a world-beating African violet. Always remember that for a new hybrid to be worth while and successful it should be different in some way, or have improved qualities over other hybrids already in being. Therefore the first step towards a breeding programme is to decide on the characteristics you want in your future hybrid – and take note that foliage is just as important as flower, for they must complement each other.

In aiming for a certain type of flower to be combined with a set type of leaf, many hybrids with these characteristics must be surveyed and their growth performance known by actually growing them before the two parents are finally selected. It should also be considered that in their genetic make-up there could be a number of hidden recessive traits present, as well as the obvious dominant traits that can be seen, and that those would remain hidden until a certain cross was made within a generation.

In genetics, the total number of chromosomes carrying the genes for a complete being is represented by 2n, half being present in each of the male and female gametes. There are a total of thirty chromosomes in the make up of an African violet, fifteen in the male gamete (the pollen grain) and fifteen in the female gamete (the egg cell). These fifteen pairs of chromosomes carry all the genes controlling the hereditary traits of the parents. During hybridization, fertilization of the seed parent is only complete when its fifteen chromosomes pair up with the fifteen from the pollen parent to give the 2n number.

Each gene controlling a characteristic or trait is either dominant, represented by a capital letter such as 'B', or recessive, represented by the lower case of the letter, in this case 'b'. A pair of genes would be shown as 'BB' for double dominant, 'Bb' as carrying the hidden recessive trait, or as 'bb' bringing the recessive trait to the fore. In African violets, as in all plants, genes of certain colours are dominant to others, and likewise leaf and flower types have dominant or recessive genes. Therefore in crossing two hybrids some surprises are likely to appear.

In hybridization, one gene for colour from the egg cell pairs up with one gene from the pollen grain. If both parents are double dominant for blue, then all the progeny will be double dominant for blue. However, if one parent is double dominant and the other is, say, one dominant for blue and one recessive for red, then although all the progeny would be blue-flowered, half of them would carry the recessive red gene that could appear in later generations. This is probably better understood by following the gene pattern below:

	BB	×	Bb	will give:	
BB	Bb		BB	Bb	first
(1)	(2)		(3)	(4)	generation

This shows that all the progeny would be blue-flowered, although half of them would carry the gene for red flowers. In further crossing within the first generation, by crossing (1) and (3) double dominance for blue is achieved, and any further crossing within their progeny would continue this dominance. However, crossing (2) and (4) of the first generation red-coloured flowers would appear thus:

	Bb	×	Bb	will give:	
	(2)		(4)		
BB	Bb		bB	bb	second
(5)	(6)		(7)	(8)	generation

This shows that in the resulting second generation, a quarter are double dominant, half carry the red gene, and a quarter would have red flowers. Any further crossing within this second generation could increase the percentage of red-flowered hybrids. Taking into account all the paired genes for all the different traits on a chromosome, it is evident that there could be many differences in the siblings.

As stated, the colour blue is dominant to all other colours, but if a blue gene is not present a recessive colour will become dominant: for example it is known that lavender is dominant to red and pink; red is dominant to pink; and all colours are dominant to white. Similarly there are dominant and recessive traits in flower and foliage types. In flowers the original *Saintpaulia* species type is dominant to star type; double to single; geneva edge to coloured edge; and fringed edge to plain edge. In foliage, girl leaf is dominant to boy leaf; ruffled margin to plain margin; plain or tailored leaf to spooned; red-backed leaf to green and silver-backed.

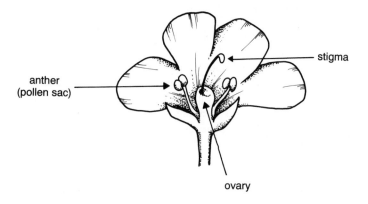

anther
(pollen sac)

stigma

ovary

Female and male parts of a flower.

Thus, crossing a double-flowered girl silver-backed leafed parent with a single-flowered boy red-backed leafed parent can, in one of the future generations, produce a double-flowered boy silver-backed leafed hybrid. And so on, with all the different types of flower and foliage. Therefore it can be understood that it might take a long time before the desired objectives in flower and foliage are achieved in a hybrid. At the same time it is possible that a number of worthwhile hybrids could appear during the breeding programme, ones that could be used. With this in mind, if when part-way through a breeding programme an interesting new trait appears in a plant which the hybridist would like to establish further in the programme, back crossing is used. This is done by using the pollen from the new hybrid to fertilize both the original parents; you then continue working with the two new programmes that result.

One difficulty in choosing parents is that the parentage of very few of the modern hybrids is published by the hybridists, and even when the parents *are* known, there may be very little information regarding the grandparents and earlier breeding; so genetically the parents are closed books. Only a hybridist with many years' experience of keeping records concerning his own breeding programmes could have an inkling of what might result from crossing two of his own hybrids, in his attempts to achieve his further objecives with any success.

Nevertheless, a great deal of satisfaction can be obtained by producing your very own hybrids through selecting some traits that you particularly like in a plant and by crossing two of your plants to achieve this. So the next step is to understand the relevant parts of a flower and their function. The female organ is the pistil made by the ovary containing the ovules or

Label showing details of cross.

egg cells, the style and the stigma; the male organ is the stamen made by the filiment and the anther containing the pollen grains.

Once the decision has been made as to which plant should be the seed parent and which the pollen parent, anthers of two or three flowers of the seed parent should be carefully cut away as soon as the flower opens, to prevent self-pollination. The stigma is usually ready to accept pollen two or three days after the flower is fully open. With experience, observation of the stigma through a magnifying glass shows when it is receptive, as its mouth appears to open slightly and becomes sticky.

Anthers from the pollen parent are removed when they are ripe, usually five to seven days after the flower fully opens, and they are split open either by a thumb nail or a needle to release the pollen which is then transferred to the seed parent stigmas. The fertilized flowers are labelled with the date and the cross, and records are written up. This latter is most important. It is advisable to repeat the transfer of pollen from the pollen parent to the stigmas two days later, and it might be interesting to reverse the crossing as well.

When a pollen grain becomes attached to a stigma it sends a tube down the inside of the style into the ovary, and male and female gametes unite to produce the paired chromosomes and complete fertilization. The outward sign that this has taken place is when the ovary begins to swell with embryo seeds. Swelling will continue until the seed pod is ripe, and until then it will remain green in colour. It will also assume a certain shape: this may be long and thin, oval or round, and which one it becomes seemingly goes back to the seed-pod shapes of the species. It has been found advantageous to keep plants carrying seed pods in a slightly less humid atmosphere to encourage the pods to ripen.

The time of ripening depends upon the type of African violet, a miniature taking about three months whilst a standard will take five to six months. Once it does ripen it will possibly begin to look translucent, and also fawnish in colour, and the pedicel begins to wither. When this happens the seed pod should be removed, placed on a fold of paper and kept in a warm position to complete the drying process, when its skin will be hard. The seed pod should now be opened with great care over a piece

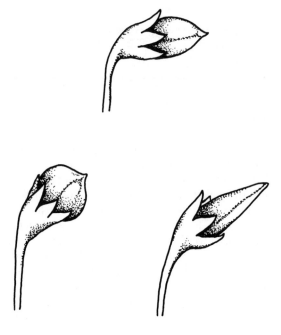

Types of seed pod.

of white paper to collect the seed, and this should either be sown immediately or kept in a cool, dry place. The dried seed pod may also be kept unopened in paper and stored in a closed jar in the salad drawer of a refrigerator. Whichever method of storing is used, it is important that the seed is clearly labelled.

When sowing the seed, it is advisable to use only half of the supply; then if that sowing is lost there is always a second chance. Viability of the seed, although possibly reducing with time, can definitely be said to last for around two years provided the seed is stored in a closed jar in the salad drawer of a refrigerator. The number of seeds in a pod depends upon the type of African violet, and may vary from about fifty to more than three hundred.

The procedure from sowing seed to potting seedlings is described in Propagation (see p. 76). What must be emphasized is that every seedling must be carried through to flowering so that the best may be selected for growing on; only then can its potential either as a probable hybrid for release, or as a parent in the next stage of the hybridization programme be assessed. If it is to be considered for release, propagation by leaf must be carried out through a minimum of three generations to prove its stability in flower type and colour, and in foliage type, and whether it is a good or better hybrid. It must be an improvement on, or different in some way to previous hybrids to be accepted for registration by the AVSA. This may mean that out of an initial selection of up to one hundred seedlings per generation of a breeding programme, in the end only one would be considered for release to the public. Thus the hybridist must obviously be ruthless in discarding seedlings that do not come up to expectations, otherwise the market would be flooded with mediocre African violets.

Regarding the breeding of variegated foliage African violets, the important fact to remember is that the seed parent must have variegated foliage for the progeny to be variegates. This is because the gene for variegated foliage is carried only by the ovule or egg cell of the seed parent. Thus the pollen parent may be a variegate or even all-green leaved, but whichever it was, there would be no doubt of the progeny being variegated; in fact some hybridists prefer to use all-green leaved hybrids as pollen parents when breeding for variegation.

All this procedure may appear to be long drawn out and complicated to someone who just thinks it might be fun to cross two plants and get some seed. And why shouldn't they do just that? To those who are very enthusiastic, however, it is the natural progressive step towards producing *the* African violet that everyone would want to have in their collection.

Whether light-hearted or serious, all growers would begin in the easiest way, that is, by crossing two single-flowered hybrids. With single flowers the stigma and anthers are obvious to see and to work with; yet the progeny are often surprisingly different to the parents because of the hidden traits in their make-up. Later they would progress to using double flowers, all the while gaining that necessary experience as they strive to achieve their ultimate desired objective.

8

PESTS, DISEASES AND DISORDERS

INSECT PESTS

Unfortunately African violets are not immune to attack by insect pests: some can be easily controlled, others with great difficulty, and a few not at all. The best method of beginning any control is by checking for symptoms of infestation every time a plant is handled in any way, for example when watering and grooming. Early recognition of pest attack and action to eradicate it will greatly lessen the problem.

Types of Control

There are two types of **chemical control** of pests, although it may be that both cannot be used against all insect pests. *Contact insecticides* act as the term implies, by the active agents coming into contact with the pest. This type is sprayed thoroughly onto all surfaces of a plant, and includes malathion, pyrethrins and resmethrin. *Systemic insecticides* are absorbed by a plant through the leaves and roots. They may be sprayed onto a plant to be taken in through the leaves, or watered onto the compost to be taken up by the roots. This type makes the sap of a plant poisonous to sucking insects and includes dimethoate. Additional caution should be taken with systemic insecticides as they appear to have a phyto-toxic effect on a plant when bright light falls on one which has been treated; therefore light intensity around such plants should be greatly reduced as a precaution for about one week after treatment. African violets under fluorescent lighting should be left without the lights, and plants on window-sills should be taken off and placed in a very shaded position.

Whenever using chemical insectitudes *always* read the label and follow the directions closely. Make sure the chemical can be used on African violets safely, and never be tempted either to increase the recommended dosage or to decrease it. The former is most likely to kill the plant as well as the pest, and the latter will only improve the pest's resistance to the chemical, and if that happens the resistance is passed on to later gener-ations of the pest, making it very difficult indeed to kill.

Insecticides are manufactured for use on plants in different ways. They may be sold as liquid concentrates that have to be diluted before treatment; as dusts for mixing with compost or dusting over foliage; and there is a systemic one in the form of an impregnated cardboard pin that is inserted into compost. There are also the contact-acting natural fatty acids which come in the form of soaps for spraying onto plants. Whatever the form an insecticide takes, always use protective measures for your own safety; at the very least wear rubber gloves when handling the chemicals.

Biological control is now available for use against many pests, whereby a live predator or organism is used specifically to combat one pest. These controls are normally for use under glass but in certain circumstances, such as in a plant room, they may be used in the home. Bear in mind that predators starve and die once they have eradicated their specific pests, which means they have to be reintroduced should another attack occur. Bacillus organisms are so far not relevant to African violets.

PESTS

The following pests are the ones which most commonly attack African violets, although you may be fortunate and never have to take control measures against some of them. Wherever possible, mention is made of biological control as well as chemical.

Aphids

There are very many aphid species, but luckily only a few attack African violets – although these tend to be difficult to eradicate. The life-cycle of the aphid is unusual, to say the least. All individuals are unmated wingless females, and yet these are capable of giving birth to up to one hundred live young during their lifetime of about thirty days; development from egg-embryo to adult takes five to six days. Even at birth these wingless females already have embryo aphids within their bodies, so that in theory it is possible for one female to produce forty-six generations in one year. It can therefore be appreciated that the label of 'spontaneous generation' aptly describes the aphid. When a food source becomes scarce and the wingless females become stressed as a result, a few winged females and winged males are born and fly off to mate and lay eggs. This usually happens in autumn and the eggs do not hatch until the following spring when the process of unmated wingless females begins again. If the eggs are laid in summer they hatch within a day or two, and more wingless females are born.

Aphids are sap-sucking insects, piercing leaves with their needle-like mouthparts and causing visible damage of speckling and pitting of leaf surfaces. The species which attacks African violets most frequently is the green one, although at times a black species may also enjoy a feed; both these are fat and juicy-looking. However, there is yet another tiny black species which looks like a spattering of sooty dust on the leaves.

Symptoms of Aphid Attack
1   Skins cast by the moulting insects remain on the African violet leaves and look like whitish-coloured insects. In fact these skins are often taken to be live whitefly.
2   Live aphids can be seen on leaves, and are difficult to pick off because their mouthparts are held firmly in the leaf.
3   Honeydew, which is readily produced by the aphids, makes lower stalks and leaves sticky. The surface the plant stands on will also be sticky.
4   Black sooty mould appears on the lower leaves and feeds on the honeydew.

Control of Aphids   A chemical insecticide containing pirimicarb is an aphid specific, killing aphids but without harming beneficial insects. It is a contact insecticide, that is, it has to wet the aphid; it also has a slight vapour action spreading around the plant. Other contact insecticides containing rotenone or pyrethrins may also be used against aphids. Besides these there are biological controls for aphids, namely larvae that either parasitize them or kill and feed on them; however, the aphid population needs to be small, and a minimum temperature of 50°F (10°C) is required for the control to be effective. Large aphid populations should be reduced before biological control is attempted, by spraying with either a soft soap solution or a contact insecticide. If the latter is used, introduction of the predator should be delayed for seven days.

Broad Mite
This mite, *Polyphagotarsonemus latus*, attacks the older, outer leaves of African violets by feeding on both the upper and lower surfaces, when they inject toxic chemicals into the leaves. Broad mite cannot be seen with the naked eye. They are colourless when young, turning to amber then to dark green as adults. Female mites can lay up to five eggs a day, but they have a short life-span.

Symptoms of Attack
1   The leaves turn yellowish in colour and become brittle, with the edges curling under.
2   The underside of the leaves develops a bronzed appearance.
3   The flowers become distorted and discoloured.
4   Damaged leaves continue to grow, but they crack and split, giving a ragged appearance.

Control of Broad Mite It is difficult to control an attack in the UK because the miticide Dicofol is not available to the amateur grower. As a suggestion worth trying, control could be attempted by removing all the outer layers of leaves, thus reducing the plant to a centre crown. A more difficult control method, and one that could also be a drastic treatment, is to submerge the entire plant, compost and pot in a container of water held at precisely 110°F (43°C) for fifteen minutes. This temperature must be very closely controlled and not allowed to go above or below by even a fraction of a degree; hence the difficulty of the treatment for the amateur who is unlikely to have access to such control equipment.

Cyclamen Mite

Steneotarsonemus pallidus is the scourge of all African violet growers. It cannot be seen with the naked eye as it is barely one hundredth of an inch long, and by the time the damage it causes is noticeable the plant is lost – moreover, not only that plant but the whole collection would be infested. Under a microscope, adults can be seen to be oval in shape, amber to tan in colour and they glisten as if oily. They live for about one month, and females will lay about one hundred eggs in that time. These mites also inject toxic chemicals as they feed on the young leaves of the centre crown.

Symptoms of Attack
1   The centre crown leaves remain very small, they stop growing and appear very hairy because of the damage caused to live tissue.
2   The centre crown becomes grey, brown or yellowish in colour and dries up.
3   The centre crown leaves become twisted, bunched and brittle.
4   Flower stalks appear short, thick and deformed, the flowers fail to develop and those that do have streaks and/or blotches of darker hues.

Control of Cyclamen Mite Once again chemical control is by thorough spraying with Dicofol which is not available in the UK to the amateur. All the authors can suggest is the procedure they used when their collections were attacked by cyclamen mite. It is drastic and heart-breaking: every African violet is destroyed by incineration, whether mature or plantlet or leaf; the compost also goes into the incinerator. All pots and trays are soaked thoroughly in a very hot, strong bleach solution and left overnight, then thoroughly rinsed in hot water. All shelves where plants have been standing must be wiped down with a strong solution of bleach, then washed with hot water. And as a final precaution, no African violet should be brought into the home for at least three to four months to ensure that there is no re-infestation. It is quite possible that cyclamen mite is often brought into the home on cut flowers from the garden or florist.

Foliar Mealy Bugs

Several species of foliar mealy bug can attack African violets, but the most likely is *Planococcus citri*. However, all are about 0.25in (0.5cm) long, soft bodied, and covered with a white, waxy webbing that protects them from drying out. Their life-cycle is six to eight weeks, and the wingless females are mated by winged males that die immediately afterwards. The females may bear either live young, or lay two hundred to four hundred eggs in a mass; these usually hatch in five to ten days depending upon temperature. The young feed for four to five weeks, moving around a plant looking for suitable sites, and pupate on the plants, the adults emerging in one to two weeks. They excrete a large volume of honeydew.

Symptoms of Attack
1   Small, creamy-white, mealy cotton wool patches appear, normally found on leaves or in leaf axils.
2   Cream-coloured grubs or larvae can be seen within the wool.
3   Leaves become yellow and the plants wilt.
4   Buds and flowers drop prematurely.

Control of Foliar Mealy Bug   A small infestation may be cleaned off plants using a cotton wool swab soaked in methylated spirit, ensuring that the larva inside each waxy woolly patch is removed. Heavy infestations may be treated by spraying the foliage thoroughly or drenching the compost with a systemic insecticide containing dimethoate, or spraying the foliage thoroughly with either a malathion or resmethrin solution. After treatment, frequent inspection of plants should be made to ensure the control is effective. Biological control of a small infestation is possible using the predator *Cryptolaemus*, a large type of ladybird. It lays its eggs in the cluster of mealy bug eggs, and the two larvae are similar in appearance although the predator larva is larger and moves more quickly. Both the predator and its larvae feed on the mealy bug, taking several weeks to eradicate it. With heavy infestations the populations should be reduced somewhat, using either methylated spirit or soft soap, prior to the release of the predator. Once all mealy bugs have been consumed, the waxy webbing should be washed from the plant with a soft soap solution.

Soil Mealy Bugs

The most common species attacking African violets is the Pritchard mealy bug, *Rhizoecus pritchard*. Its infestation is very difficult to diagnose because it feeds on fine roots and is hidden in the compost. It is minute in size, being about half the size of a foliar mealy bug, and white in colour due to the powdery wax exuded from its body, so it can look like a fragment of perlite in the compost. In fact it can go undetected until a plant is potted on or repotted. The glassy eggs are laid ten to twenty at a time and are surrounded by waxy webbing; they hatch in one to two days and begin to feed immediately. Their life-cycle lasts two to four months, and so all stages are present in an infested plant's rootball.

Symptoms of Attack
1 Because its roots are damaged the plant cannot take up water, so it becomes limp even though the compost may be very moist.
2 Very fine white threads and the insects can be seen around the roots and through the rootball.
3 Soil mealy bugs do not move even when touched with a needle.
4 A sure sign of infestation is the white waxy patches of webbing on the inside of the plant's pot.

Control of Pritchard Mealy Bug The rootball should be thoroughly drenched with a solution of either a systemic insecticide containing dimethoate, or a contact insecticide containing malathion, made up at the recommended strength. After seven to ten days all compost should be washed away from the roots with hot water, the roots washed thoroughly and the plant potted up in a clean pot with fresh compost. It should be stood on a separate saucer away from other plants and given extra attention for the next three or four weeks whilst the roots are recovering. There are reports of the successful use of diatomaceous earth mixed in with the compost to control soil mealy bug. This material is the skeletal remains of diatoms and the fragments have very sharp edges; it appears that these cut the soil mealy bugs so severely that they die.

Red Spider Mite
This pest should be a rarity on African violets because of the fairly high relative humidity around the plants. However, *Tetranychus urticae* can transfer from other nearby houseplants or from cut flowers from a florist by the thread that all spiders produce. Red spider mite is found on the underside of leaves or around young growth, and it is a prolific breeder in dry conditions. It can be reddish, amber or green in colour. In heavy infestations it can easily be seen moving fairly rapidly through its webbing.

Symptoms of Attack
1 Leaves become speckled and yellowing, and will drop.
2 Red spider mites can be seen in their webbing on leaves and young shoots.

Control of Red Spider Mite   The easiest method of control is to maintain the relative humidity levels around the plants. Chemical sprays containing perimiphos-methyl and/or pyrethrins may be used, the former having a translaminer activity so it reaches the under-surface of leaves where this pest prefers to be. There is also a predator mite, *Phytoseiulus persimilis*, which will control red spider mite, although the temperature must exceed 50°F (10°C) for it to be effective. It is a voracious feeder and will devour the pests fairly quickly. However, do not use a systemic insecticide before introducing this predator.

Scale Insects

There are two species of scale insect that are likely to attack African violets: the fern scale *Pinnaspis aspidistrae*, and the brown soft-scale *Coccus hesperidum*. The scale is wax, or resin, secreted by the body of the insect which lives under it. Fern scale is termed 'armoured' because it has a hard covering; the females are light-coloured and pear-shaped, and lose their legs and antennae soon after hatching so that for their remaining lifetime they are immobile. Fern scale males are long and narrow in shape and winged. Brown soft-scale adult females are brown in colour, spherical in shape, and wingless; they reproduce by egg laying or live birth, and retain their legs. Brown soft-scale males are most likely to be winged, white in colour, and long and narrow in shape resembling small gnats. The hatchlings are called 'crawlers' and are very active, moving through a plant looking for a feeding site to settle and secrete their scale. All scale insects excrete honeydew.

Symptoms of Attack
1   Honeydew will be evident on the lower leaves and the surface on which the plant is standing.
2   Small, discoloured spots appear on the upper surface of a leaf indicating where scales are attached on the underside.
3   A discoloured and pitted area appears on the underside of a leaf where the scale is attached near to the main vein.

Control of Scale Insects   Very light infestations may be dealt with by using a cotton wool swab or cocktail stick, removing the scale and the insect physically. A swab may be soaked in methylated spirit to help in this operation. With this method, frequent and close inspection of plants is a necessity. Chemical control is by spraying with an insecticide containing dimethoate, malathion or permethrin. A repeat dosage is recommended seven to ten days later in order to catch any surviving hatchlings or nymphs.

Sciarid Fly

More commonly known as the 'fungus gnat', this is really considered to be a nuisance pest; it is very frequently present in composts that have been stored outdoors and left open to the elements, for example in garden centres. Sciarid flies are the tiny black flies often seen around plants. They breed in moist compost containing a high percentage of organic matter, the females laying minute white eggs in batches of about thirty at a time; these hatch in four to six days, and the larvae are very mobile, choosing fungi or decaying organic matter for their food. At five to fourteen days old the larvae pupate in or on the compost, the adults emerging five to six days later. The adult flies feed on nectar. Sciarid flies very rarely damage African violets; only when there is a very large population of larvae in a compost with very little organic matter will they feed on plant roots.

Symptoms of Attack
1   Tiny black flies which can be seen around plants.

Control of Sciarid Flies   Normally very good control is achieved by placing yellow-coloured sticky traps among the plants: these traps are in fact no more than small strips of yellow plastic, coated with a non-toxic glue, yellow being an attractive colour to flying insects. In the event of a heavy infestation, a drench of malathion may be used. Over-watering of plants tends to encourage sciarid flies. One other means of control is an insectivorous plant such as a pinguicula; these have sticky leaves specifically designed to catch the tiny flies, which they then ingest.

Springtails
This is another nuisance pest, often to be found in the saucers of plants with very wet compost. However, even when present in very large numbers springtails do not damage African violets; it is more that they are unsightly and do not please judges of African violets if they are seen in the saucers. Springtails are about 0.125in (0.3cm) long and whitish in colour, and they have a noticeable jumping action due to the spring-like structure which is normally folded beneath their bodies; this is not used when just walking about, but when the insect is disturbed it flicks it along. Adults deposit large batches of eggs in compost; the hatchlings resemble the adults, and growth is rapid, the insects reaching maturity in two or three weeks. They feed on very damp, decaying organic material.

Control of Springtails   Plants should not be over-watered, although springtails are very often taken as an indication that African violets are growing in compost of the right moisture with good drainage, and that they are well oxygenated at the roots. When plants are to be entered in a competitive show, a soil drench of pyrethrins a few days before the show is advisable.

Symphylids

These are also termed a nuisance pest, as they do not cause any actual damage to African violets. They have the appearance of tiny white centipedes, being no longer than 0.4in (1cm), but they have only twelve legs, long antennae and no eyes. The females lay clusters of twelve to twenty eggs in compost and the hatchlings resemble the adults, although they are smaller and have fewer legs. The life-cycle from egg to adult takes three to six weeks. They are rarely seen except when the rootball is removed from its pot, and then great numbers of them may be seen moving rapidly through it.

Control of Symphylids   Only when there are vast numbers of symphylids present is any control needed, and then it is easily carried out by drenching the compost with an insecticide containing permethrin, pyrethrins or resmethrin.

Thrips

There are many species of this insect pest but the most significant as far as African violets in the UK are concerned are the western flower thrips *Frankliniella occidentalis*, and the onion thrips *Thrips tabaci*. The adults are tiny, less than 0.1in (0.2cm) long, torpedo-shaped with narrow, fringed and feathered wings, and yellow in colour. The females lay their eggs either in crevices and cracks in the tissue of the plant, or into the tissue itself. The eggs hatch into translucent larvae and feed for about fifteen days before pupating. They feed by scraping and rasping at the leaves to suck sap, and they also feed on pollen grains. Pupae often drop down onto the compost and emerge as adults after three to nine days, depending upon the temperature; for example at 68°F (20°C) the life-cycle from egg to adult is twenty-two days. Because adult thrips are so small and are able to fly, they very readily come into the home through open doors and windows, on cut flowers brought in from florist or garden, on clothes, hands and pet animals. In fact it is virtually impossible to keep them out of any home and away from African violet collections. Whilst a very small infestation may go unnoticed and die out, the damage resulting from a large infestation can be seen quite easily.

Symptoms of Attack
1   Pollen scattered on flowers and leaves. Check the flowers by vibrating one, and watch for tiny scuttling insects.
2   The flower colour becomes streaked and has a silvered appearance.
3   Leaves are discoloured and spotted by faeces, rasped areas are silvered and scarred.
4   Heavy infestations mean that pests are feeding continually, and this may cause curled or deformed leaf growth.

Control of Thrips Rapid chemical control in the home is impossible because nicotine is not available for this purpose, as being excessively dangerous. Therefore the amateur must use other means. At the first sign of infestation, *all* flowers and buds must be removed from *all* the plants in the collection whether they show symptoms or not, because pollen is the main food source. No buds should be allowed to grow on the plants for at least one month. After all the flowers and buds have been taken off, the plants should be sprayed thoroughly and the compost drenched with an insecticide containing perimiphos-methyl – and remember to reduce the light intensity for the plants, as this agent has systemic action. After one month, buds can be allowed to grow; however when flowering commences, checks for thrips must be repeated and if any are found, once again flowers and buds must be taken off and insecticidal treatment repeated. Close inspection for reinfestation must continue.

Biological control is now available with the predator mite *Amblyseius cucumeris*. The mite feeds on only the youngest thrips' larvae, devouring one or two a day, so it must be reintroduced at weekly intervals until no adult thrips are seen to emerge. This predator can be supplied as a breeding culture that should be placed among plants.

Vine Weevil

Otiorhynchus sulcatus is a very rare visitor to plants growing in the home, but it is often found in the garden and so could come inside. The adult beetle is flightless, nocturnal and easily recognizable by its prominent snout. If seen, it is best to kill it before it can lay eggs. Nearly all the adults are female, so reproduction is parthenogenic; from spring to early summer the female will lay up to one thousand eggs, although thankfully not all hatch. The larva emerges after about two weeks and is easily identified by its 0.25in (0.5cm) long, fat, curled, creamy-coloured body and very noticeable black or dark brown head. It will feed for around three months on the roots of plants, and then pupate in the compost, the adults emerging the following spring.

Symptoms of Attack
1   The plant suddenly collapses and will be seen to have no roots.
2   Larvae will be found in the compost.

Control of Vine Weevil Dispose of the compost safely – do not put it out into the garden. The crown of the plant may be re-rooted after thorough washing of the damaged stem with hot water. Mix the powder gamma-BHC into the compost being used for re-rooting; inspect frequently for any subsequent root damage. When handling any compost containing the insecticide it is highly advisable to wear rubber gloves. Biological control can be carried out by the parasitic nematode *Heterorhabolitis megidis*. A culture of the nematode is added to water and poured onto the compost which should have been watered the day before. The compost temperature must be in excess of 50°F (10°C) for the nematode to become active against the vine weevil larvae, which will die in about three to five weeks – the warmer the temperature the quicker the action. Biological control should not be attempted until more than six weeks have elapsed since treatment with gamma-BHC.

Whitefly
Very few of the whitefly species attack African violets, but those that do can produce a heavy infestation quite quickly. The adult is less than 0.1in (0.2cm) long and entirely covered with a milky-white waxy powder. It has two pairs of wings, and both adults and young have mouthparts that enable them to suck sap from the leaves of plants. The females lay eggs in batches of about forty at a time on the backs of leaves, and the eggs hatch in four to twelve days; a hatchling takes the form of a crawling nymph that is nearly transparent. Once settled on a feeding site, the nymph moults and becomes legless; it is covered with a waxy scale. It will continue to feed for twenty-eight to thirty days until it emerges as an adult fly; the adults live for about forty days. Both scale nymph and adult secrete quantities of honeydew.

Symptoms of Attack
1   Clouds of tiny whiteflies which arise when plants are disturbed.
2   Honeydew and sooty mould are present on a plant's lower leaves, and on the surface where plants are standing.
3   Nymph scales can be seen on the backs of leaves.
4   Plant leaves become yellow.

Control of Whitefly   Control of this pest can be difficult. Thorough spraying, especially of the undersides of leaves, with an insecticide containing pyrethrins, permethrin or perimiphos-methyl will only control the adult population, therefore the treatment must be repeated every four days until adults cease to emerge. Some control of adults may be achieved by the use of sticky glue traps hanging amongst the plants; the adults are attracted to these by their colour.

Biological control of whitefly is by the tiny parasitic wasp *Encarsia formosa*, which to complete its own life-cycle is entirely dependent on the pest because it lays its eggs in the nymph scales on the backs of leaves. A scale will be seen to turn black as the wasp's larva consumes the nymph, so that an *Encarsia* wasp finally emerges from the scale instead of a whitefly. Temperatures in excess of 50°F (10°C) are needed for *Encarsia* to begin to be effective, and the best temperature range is 65° to 85°F (18° to 30°C). When control by *Encarsia* is proposed, insecticides containing pyrethrins should not be used for seven days before their introduction, and permethrin and perimiphos-methyl should not be used for at least three weeks. Sticky glue traps should be removed from the plants so that *Encarsia* are not attracted to them.

The following cannot be repeated often enough; ignore it at your peril! Always remember that insecticides are not only insect killers, they can also be very harmful to humans, other animals and plants. Therefore be very careful to read the label correctly; check that the chemical will not harm your plants; be quite sure not to increase or decrease the rec-ommended dosages, and to give them at the times directed; and make sure that all protective precautions are properly taken.

When using biological control measures by predator, always follow the directions, and do not use chemical insecticides at the same time.

DISEASES

African violets are comparatively tough plants that are not prone to attack by fungal diseases; if infection does strike it is usually as a result of bad cultivation on the part of the grower. In many instances control of the infection does not entail the use of chemical fungicides, though when necessary those with a contact or systemic action may be used. Fungicides are supplied in the form of liquid concentrates for dilution with water, or as powders to be applied either dry or to be mixed with water.

The following diseases are the ones most likely to be met by the grower of African violets.

Botrytis
This grey mould fungus is always a secondary infection as it attacks plant tissues already damaged. It appears as grey fluffy needles on stems and leaves and spreads very rapidly, so that when seen it is really too late to use a fungicide treatment to save the plant. Therefore the plant should be incinerated, and its pot and the area where it was positioned thoroughly cleaned. Botrytis rarely transfers from plant to plant unless it is by hand-ling another plant after the infected one.

Crown, Stem and Root Rot
These infections usually appear when cold conditions prevail, and when African violets are over-potted in wet compost.

Crown rot is the result of allowing water to remain within the young leaves of the crown. The leaves become brown, soft and mushy and the infection will spread to the surrounding leaves; if left, it will continue to spread into the stem. **Root rot** causes a plant to wilt and collapse because there are no healthy roots to sustain it. Usually the first thought when a plant is seen to wilt is to water it, which in this case only increases the problem because the compost is already much too wet.

Control
1 Any water lodging in a crown should be mopped away with a soft tissue and the crown allowed to dry.
2 Judicial watering should be carried out with either the contact fungicide benomyl, or the systemic fungicides bupirimate and triforine.
3 Affected leaves of the crown, provided they are not badly affected, should be dusted with green or yellow sulphur dust.
4 With root rot, provided the rot has not extended into the stem, the entire rootball should be cut away and the crown re-rooted.

Mildew
The fungal infection of mildew – more often spoken of as powdery mildew – appears on the buds, flowers and leaves of African violets as a white powdery deposit. It is usually seen when plants are crowded together either in cold, wet conditions or when it is hot, still and excessively humid. The infection spreads rapidly through a collection and requires quick action.

Control
1 Flowers and buds should be taken off the plants and the foliage sprayed with the fungicide benomyl or watered with one containing bupirimate and triforine.
2 Plants should be placed more widely apart for better air circulation.
3 In hot weather use an electric fan to give gentle air circulation.

Pythium
Provided the compost is well pasteurized, this fungal disease should not affect African violets. However, it is such a devastating infection that we feel it should be brought to the notice of growers. It is a soil- or compost-borne fungus and is fatal to plants. Its spores are able to survive for a long time before they come into contact with a host, and then they grow hyphae which penetrate the roots or stems of the plant. Pythium also produces motile spores which will infect other plants standing on the same capillary matting or tray.

Symptoms of the disease are as follows: The centre crown of an infected plant shrivels, its leaves begin to look whitish with brown edges, and soon afterwards the whole plant turns black and dies. Fungicides appear to have little or no effect on the problem, although it might be worth trying them.

Control   In real terms, the sole control is that the remains of the plant and any capillary matting should be incinerated, and the pots, trays and shelves cleaned very thoroughly with a strong solution of bleach. As an added precaution to prevent re-infection, no African violets should be grown in the area previously infected for several weeks. When restocking with leaves or plants, these should be watered carefully with a commercial preparation of copper sulphate and ammonium carbonate, the solution made up at the recommended strength.

Sooty Mould
This fungus grows on the honeydew excreted by pests. It should not be a problem because action should have been taken against the pests before the honeydew became infected. If it is present, however, the affected leaves should be taken off the plants, or if it is only just showing, the leaves can be washed with warm water containing a few drops of a liquid detergent.

White Mould on Compost
Inexperienced growers are often worried when they see a white fluffy mould, or *mycelium*, on the compost surface. In fact this mould is encouraged by a compost that is too wet, and the situation is easily remedied by scraping the mycelium away and then either watering the plant with a solution of copper sulphate and ammonium carbonate, or dusting the surface of the compost with sulphur dust. The latter may appear a little messy but at least it does not make the compost any wetter than it is already.

PHYSIOLOGICAL DISORDERS

These disorders are usually caused by inefficient culture of plants or unsuitable growing conditions, both of which can be remedied. However, not all the results of the disorders can be removed by changing either culture or conditions; generaly the damage has to grow out.

White Netting on Leaves
At times a small patch of what appears to be white netting may appear on African violet leaves. It is caused by very cold water which if taken up by the roots and fed through to the leaf surface, will kill a small area of minute capillary veins. The patch does not increase in size, but neither

does it disappear with time because the damage is permanent. Thus to prevent such patches of netting disfiguring leaves, always use water either at room temperature or tepid.

Brown Spots on Leaves

If water droplets are left on leaves after spraying or accidentally after watering, the effect of very bright light falling on them is to convert them into magnifiers, and burned areas or brown spots result. To prevent this occurring, always remove any droplets with a soft tissue or allow the plant to dry, well out of the way of bright light or draughts. Brown spots also represent permanent damage.

Yellow Borders on Leaves

Plants that are kept in an ambient temperature of below 60°F (15°C) for a prolonged period are likely to show a yellowish border on their leaves with yellow spots on the edges which may also curl under. These symptoms are signs of chill and are permanent. As the damaged outside layer of leaves will not recover its good green colour, it should be removed. This disorder is more likely to be seen towards the end of winter in plants that are kept in a room that is not heated overnight; it is therefore good practice to keep plants a little warmer if at all possible.

Yellow Edges on Leaves

Yellow edges and pale green leaves may also be the result of under-feeding. This disorder can happen at any time of the year and so should not be confused with the yellow borders caused by chilling. Feeding with a high nitrogen fertilizer at half the recommended strength at every watering for four weeks should improve the condition; an indication of this is that the leaves become darker green.

Fertilizer Burn

Obviously this is caused by over-feeding, symptomized by the young leaves in the centre of the crown bunching together and their hairs appearing to be brown-tipped because the fertilizer salts which exude from the leaves crystallize on the hairs. Unsightly permanent damage to these leaves will be done, but they should not be removed until they have grown out. Meanwhile, flush the compost with copious amounts of warm water to wash out excess fertilizer, and also wash the centre crown with warm water, drying it afterwards with a soft tissue. Any later watering should be with small amounts of plain tepid water to lessen the possibility of root rot, and no fertilizer should be given for four to six weeks. Then very weak feeding should commence, and once the condition has been corrected normal feeding should begin.

Incorrect pH

Initially this disorder may appear to have the same symptoms as cyclamen mite attack in that the leaves in the centre crown cease to grow and have a bunched appearance. However, it is the easiest to diagnose because all that is necessary is for the pH of the compost to be checked by a meter, which will show whether it is too acidic or too alkaline.

This disorder is rarely suffered by enthusiastic growers and exhibitors, because they root prune and repot their plants so frequently. Normally this procedure is carried out every six months on standard and large-sized hybrids, and every three or four months on miniature and semi-miniature hybrids. For the grower with just a few plants on the window-sill, root pruning and repotting should be done at least once a year in spring; that way there should be no problems with incorrect pH.

Vapour Poisoning

This is not brought about either by bad culture or by unsuitable conditions, but we think it should be brought to the notice of growers as we know of several instances when it has occurred. New timber is sometimes treated with preservatives and fire retardents or fire-proofing chemicals, and poisoning happens when such timber is built into a house in any quantity. Odourless vapour can be released from it for some considerable time and will seriously affect any African violets in its vicinity. It appears not to affect certain other houseplants.

The plants will cease to grow and then they will wither away from the outside leaves. Often at this stage botrytis will set in and the plants will die. Nothing can be done at any time for the plants affected, but if the grower wishes to raise African violets in the future, the rooms must be continually ventilated and aired for several months before plants can be brought back in. Hot temperatures increase the rate of vapour release, so that its effect may appear to begin only in spring and summer. To ascertain when it is safe to grow a new collection again, two or three healthy but expendable plants should be grown in the rooms for several weeks and closely watched for any further signs of vapour poisoning.

Although the pests and diseases that have been listed may be rather daunting, readers should be neither frightened of, nor discouraged from growing African violets. It is highly unlikely that they will meet with all, or even any of the aforementioned pests and diseases, provided they inspect their plants frequently, and inspection becomes an automatic procedure when watering and grooming is carried out, and obviously that is frequently. Therefore any infestation or infection is detected early and can be dealt with immediately.

Quarantine

This is a subject that the authors never stop impressing on African violet enthusiasts. It seems to us that most growers dismiss quarantine as a lot of fuss over nothing – that is, until they suffer a monumental loss of plants. That happened to both of us many years ago, and we have tried ever since to ensure that it never happens again.

All new plants, not only African violets, coming into the home should be kept in quarantine – that is, completely away from any collection – for a minimum of eight weeks in case they are inadvertently carrying pests or disease. The new plants should be attended to *after* all the other plants in the home, and should have their own watering can, again as a precaution against transferring any pest or disease. If it is impossible to isolate them in a room away from the main collection of plants, then they could be enclosed in a large aquarium tank that can be sealed for the necessary period of time.

Wherever new plants come from, whether from friends, nurseries, garden centres or florists, they should *always* be placed in quarantine. This may seem an excessively cautious course of action to take, but we can assure you, once an entire collection has been infested or infected from new plants, the grower will ever after err on the safe side. It is always better to be safe than sorry.

9

INCREASING A COLLECTION

EXCHANGING HYBRIDS

Once a person is dedicated to growing African violets, he will be determined to enlarge his collection and this can be done by exchanging leaves of named hybrids with friends far and wide. This creates the problem of how to send leaves through the postal service in order that they arrive safely and in good condition for propagation, one which is solved by proper handling and packaging prior to mailing.

Plants from which leaves are to be taken should be watered the day before they are to be removed so that the leaves are crisp. Once taken from the plant, just the bottom of each leaf stalk should be trimmed with a sharp-bladed knife to prevent any damaged cells beginning to rot in transit. The trimming for propagation is left to the person receiving the leaves. When arrival at their destination is expected to be in one or two days, each leaf should be put into an individual polythene bag, its top folded over and kept in place by an adhesive label with the name of the leaf on it. When travelling time is expected to be four to six days, a little extra help is needed for the leaves to arrive in good condition. Thus, before a leaf is put into a small polythene bag, a small square of paper tissue is wrapped around the end of the trimmed stalk and then just moistened with water; it should not be made sodden. Then the bag is folded over and labelled.

However long or short the journey, the bagged leaves should be packed into a strong cardboard box, layered between either shredded paper or polystyrene chips. When the package arrives at its destination some of the leaves may be a little limp; these should be laid between wet kitchen paper towelling and left overnight, because moisture from the towelling can be absorbed by the leaf blades. The next morning the leaves should have crisped up and they can be potted up in the normal manner. It is not advisable to stand limp leaves in a small jar of water, because in this condition the leaf stalk is not capable of taking up sufficient water to make the leaf crisp enough for propagation, even if the stalk has been recut.

Weather conditions should also be taken into consideration: thus under no circumstances should leaves be mailed out on very hot or very cold days.

IMPORTING AFRICAN VIOLETS

Of course, the very enthusiastic grower must now look to overseas nurseries, for there are few opportunities to obtain really new named hybrids in the UK. The first step is to write for catalogues from nurseries abroad which advertise in specialist magazines. Our experience of this is mainly from the USA and Canada, but there are other nurseries around the world. An import licence may be necessary for importing from some countries; this information can be obtained from your local Ministry of Agriculture, Fisheries and Food office. An import licence is not required for plant material coming from the USA and Canada. However, all incoming African violet leaves and plants from anywhere in the world must be accompanied by a phytosanitary certificate supplied by the exporting country's Agricultural Department. This must state that the plant material is free of pest infestation and disease after inspection by an official of the department. There may be a charge for such a certificate, but without it any plant material is confiscated by HM Customs.

It is worth paying the nursery the extra charges for sending your plant material express mail which normally takes three to four days, rather than ordinary air mail which may take eight to ten days: obviously the leaves or plants will arrive in much better condition. Other possible charges could be imposed when the package is opened by HM Customs on entry into the UK. All these costs should be considered carefully when deciding to import African violets, because they do greatly increase the cost of buying from abroad.

Any nursery despatching African violets to another country takes great care with its packaging, and can be relied upon to supply good, healthy plant material; even so, it is still advisable to quarantine any leaves or plants in a covered unheated propagator once they are potted up. This will also help them to recover from their journey. And it is always good policy to write to the nursery to say the package has arrived safely – after all, suppliers do like to hear about the good things, as well as coping with complaints. African violet seed is also available from overseas, and does not require a phytosanitary certificate for import.

NATIONAL SOCIETY MEMBERSHIP

There is another way of obtaining new hybrids from abroad: that is to join the national society and get to know the members who regularly import leaves and plants of African violets. You will find that they are usually only too happy to share their imports with other members, and this is certainly a very much cheaper way to go about increasing a collection!

10

EXHIBITING AFRICAN VIOLETS

Many of the modern hybrids have been bred for exhibition, and they grow into a symmetrical rosette shape without much help. Those enthusiasts who want just to enter a plant into the local horticultural show will probably have bought a plant from a garden centre or a florist, and will train the occasional misaligned leaf into its correct position by using

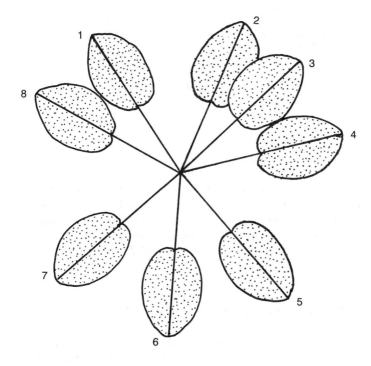

Asymmetrical leaf formation.

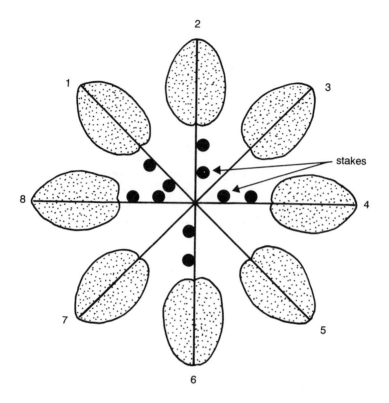

Leaves staked into a symmetrical leaf formation.

small stakes. This can usually be done easily, though at times it takes a little more work to persuade the leaves into place. When a leaf is growing very much out of position, training is done gradually. For example, on removal of the small stakes the leaf should remain where it is; then it can be re-staked nearer to its correct position and this is repeated until the plant is a symmetrical rosette.

SELECTING AN EXHIBITION PLANT

Keen exhibitors want much more from their African violets and so give much thought to selecting their show plants, generally choosing a hybrid that they know has performed well on the show table. They also know that they will probably spend at least two years growing it because they

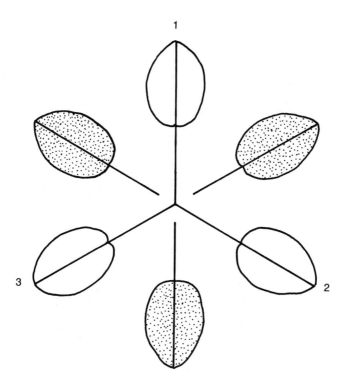

A three-leaf layer will produce a symmetrical show plant.

will begin with a carefully chosen plantlet, one which has a definite growth pattern of either three or four leaves to a layer. As the plantlet grows this pattern will be repeated, ultimately producing a symmetrical single crown of foliage where the leaf blades overlap each other in such a way that the leaf stalks cannot be seen from above.

GROOMING AN EXHIBITION PLANT

Once the selected plantlet has been potted up, grooming begins by cleanly taking away those outside baby leaves that were the first to emerge, leaving the three- or four-leaf formation. The plantlet is grown and potted on, taking care to keep the symmetrical leaf layering so that the tips of the outer layer of leaves form a circle. In order to see this circle

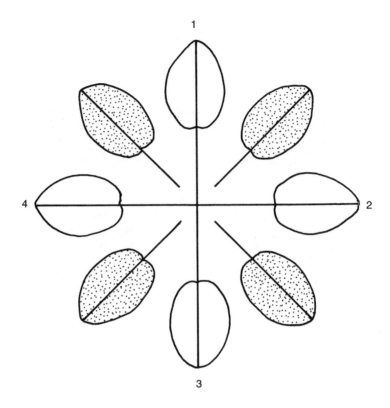

A four-leaf layer will also produce a symmetrical show plant with more closely overlapping leaves.

clearly, the plant should be stood on the floor and viewed vertically from above: like this, any leaves in the outer layer that do not conform can be easily seen and should be removed. However, before removing any leaves it is best to be absolutely sure, and the best way is to cover the suspect leaves with small squares of tissue paper so they cannot be seen. If the shape is improved the covered leaves come off the plant; if the shape has not been improved or if you are not sure, the leaves stay on the plant. This grooming is done every week or so. Leaves that definitely should be removed are those that are hidden under the outer larger leaves and cannot be seen from above. The rule is, if it cannot be seen it should not be there. All this grooming procedure continues right up until exhibition time.

GROWING AN EXHIBITION PLANT

The first step is to make sure that the plant flowers true to description, and so a first flowering is allowed; then no flowers are permitted until the foliage has grown to the size wanted. For this reason the preferred policy should be to feed for foliage growth, and fertilizers of high nitrogen should be given three times more often than the high phosphate/potash fertilizer. During this period of growth the plant should be potted on into a pot one size larger every time it appears to be under-potted. Disbudding by removing any buds as they form continues until the diameter across the single crown is the required size; from that time the plant is root pruned and repotted every five or six months. The next step is to find how long it would take the plant to progress from beginning to bud, and then up to full flower, so that when exhibition time is approaching you will know when to stop disbudding.

Whilst disbudding continues the bud stalk should not be removed entirely, but a short stub about 0.25in (0.6cm) long should be left so that a possible later, second bud may emerge from the same leaf axil. Pay attention that the stub does not begin to rot; if it does it should be removed immediately. Very rough estimates of when to stop disbudding before a show are, six weeks for single-flowered hybrids and eight weeks for double-flowered hybrids. Accurate times are obtained by observation, as the plants can be a law until themselves. When disbudding is stopped the plant should only be fed with a high phosphate/potash fertilizer.

Throughout the growth process of the plant, any sucker forming in a leaf axil must be removed; although in later growth, take care that it really *is* a sucker because some hybrids have a comparatively large pair of leaves behind the bud. However, by this time the grower should have knowledge of this fact.

Exhibition miniatures and semi-miniatures are treated in exactly the same way, except they should be root pruned and repotted every three months and they should not be disbudded. Frequently the little ones are shy to flower after disbudding so it is best to let them do their own thing. Trailing hybrids are similarly treated but it is important to realize that they must have a minimum of three branches coming from the main stem; it is even better to have more, and judicious pinching out of the growing points in the crowns will produce an exhibition plant. With so many crowns and close, short branch growth, it may be difficult for a judge to see that there is only one stem. In fact today many exhibitors grow trailers in wide shallow pans and pin down the branches so that they can root down. For exhibition purposes questions have been asked as to whether this is one plant or many, but it is now accepted as one plant. A trailer should have an even distribution of flowers coming from every crown.

As exhibition time approaches and the plant comes into flower, any flower stalks that are badly positioned should be gently eased into position between the leaves, so that when in full bloom the plant looks like a posy. That is to say, the plant should have a compact head of flowers surrounded by a ring of leaves. There are some show hybrids which cannot grow their flowers in this position, but as long as there is an abundance of blooms growing evenly over the foliage the judges will not mark the plant down.

EXHIBITION DAY

Preparing the Plant for the Show Table
A few days before the show, the plant should be inspected for blemished, scarred leaves (which should have been taken off earlier), for water marks, dust and compost particles, for flowers that have passed their best, and for seed pods. Any of these constitute a fault and if they are seen on the show table marks would be lost. Water marks can be removed by very gentle rubbing with a wet tissue or soft cloth. Dust and compost can be removed by gentle use of a small soft brush on the leaf blade, working from base to tip. Dying and faded flowers should be snipped off carefully so as not to leave a stub of pedicel, and any seed pods should be taken off. Checks should also be made that no old bud or leaf stalk stubs have been forgotten, and that the plant pot is clean without any salt scale on it. The day before the show the plant should be watered so that it will not be stressed while being exhibited, and packed into its carrier.

Transporting the Plant
The best carrier for a show plant is a strong cardboard box big enough so that no part of the plant will touch any surface, and it should be firmly supported in the box. It will be kept most securely in place by a sheet of cardboard or thin plywood cut to fit the inside diameter of the box tightly, with a central hole cut to fit halfway up the height of the plant's pot. If this is not possible, a firm nest of crushed paper or polystyrene chips should be used in the box to keep the plant firmly supported. In this way plants can be transported safely to the show.

Staging the Plant
Before the plant is placed in its show class it should be checked over again to make sure that the flowers and leaves are clean and properly positioned. It is important to ensure that a plant is showing its full potential to the judges so that they will have no difficulty in placing it as it deserves.

Judging

In the UK classes are competitive, so a first, a second and a third placing are awarded; the judges may also award a highly commended and a commended. This may seem to be difficult in circumstances where there are, say, ten or more plants in a class, but when show standards are applied it becomes obvious that certain plants will never be serious contenders because they do not perhaps have as much flower as others, or some detail has been missed in their final grooming.

The Saintpaulia and Houseplant Society publishes the standards that are used in their shows, and these are as follows:

1 Pots must be clean and not obtrusive.
2 Plants should not be over- or under-potted.
3 Plants should be clean and healthy, showing no sign of infestation or infection.
4 Saintpaulias should be single crowned unless a trailer or a species.
5 Saintpaulias should fit into one of the three size categories.
6 Foliage should be symmetrical.
7 Flower stalks should ideally emerge from towards the centre, should be fully open to count, and dying flowers should have been removed.

The judges will keep these standards in mind when inspecting and comparing the plants before them in a class, and so are able to award the prizes appropriately. Finally, the 'Best Saintpaulia in Show' must be selected from all the 'First in Class' plants.

In the Americas, judging is conducted according to a different system of merit marking and follows rules laid down by the AVSA. Points are awarded for symmetry of the plant, cultural condition, quality and quantity of flower, and also size, type and colour of the flower. The maximum number of points is one hundred: plants that are awarded a total of points from ninety to one hundred receive a blue ribbon; those from eighty to eighty-nine win a red ribbon; and seventy to seventy-nine points a white ribbon. Thus it is quite possible for most of the plants in a class to be awarded a blue ribbon; and the plant with the most points is 'Best in Class'. Finally, all the 'Best in Class' are judged again for 'Best in Show'.

After the Show

On return home, exhibited plants should have the entire flower head removed and the foliage sprayed with a broad spectrum insecticide; they should then be kept in quarantine for six to eight weeks as a precaution against any infestation collected at the show. This should not happen, but it can, one reason being the presence of plants other than African violets in the show room.

GLOSSARY

Acidic compost   A compost having a pH value of less than 7.0.

Alkaline compost   A compost having a pH value of more than 7.0.

Agar   A gelatinous substance with added nutrients and hormones used in micro-propagation or tissue culture.

Anther   The yellow sac which contains pollen. Upper part of the stamen which is the male organ of a flower.

Anthrocyanin   Pigments usually of red or pink shades found in plant tissue.

Backcross   A cross between a hybrid and both of its parents.

Bicoloured flowers   Flowers with two or more shades of one colour; often referred to as two-tone flowers.

Boy leaf   A leaf of a plain, tailored type with a smooth edge.

Calyx   Green, leaf-like cup at the base of a corolla.

Capillary action   The upward movement of water from matting or wick to a plant pot.

Chimera   Two or more genetically different tissues side by side in a plant.

Chlorophyll   The green pigmented substance in a plant essential for the process of photosynthesis.

Corolla   A term referring to all the entire lobes of a flower.

Corolla tube   The short tube formed by the base of the lobes of a flower, that sits in the calyx.

Cross   The transfer of pollen from one flower on a plant to the stigma of a flower on another plant.

Crown   The foliage and flowers of an African violet from the centre of which new leaves and buds originate.

Day-length   The hours of light needed to initiate flowering.

Disbudding   Removal of buds to delay flowering.

Division   The cutting apart of a multi-crowned plant.

Double flowers   Flowers with at least two complete layers of lobes.

Fantasy flowers   Flowers with streaks, splashes and spots of a colour different to the main colour.

Flower leaves   The small leaves growing at the top of the peduncle behind the flower cluster.

Gamete   A male reproductive cell (the pollen grain) or female reproductive cell (the ovule) holding one half of the chromosomes required for fertilization and seed production.

Geneva flower A flower having a thin white edge to its lobes.

Girl leaf A leaf with a white area extending from the leaf petiole into the leaf blade.

Humus Partially decomposed plant material.

Hybrid A plant produced by cross fertilizing two other plants.

Intergeneric cross A hybrid produced by crossing two plants from different genera.

Internode That part of the stem between two leaf nodes.

Leaf axil The angle between the upper side of a leaf petiole and the main stem of a plant. Where the leaf joins the main stem.

Leaf margin The outermost edge of a leaf blade.

Lime The chemical compound that increases the pH value of an acidic compost making it more alkaline.

Loam A natural material consisting of clay, humus and fertilizers.

Lobe Part of a flower, different to a petal because it is joined to its neighbours forming a short corolla tube; petals are individually separated.

Micro-propagation Propagation using a tiny piece of plant leaf to grow many new plants by using an agar culture in a laboratory.

Mother leaf A leaf on which plantlets grow.

Multicoloured flowers Flowers of two or more different colours.

Multi-crowned plant A plant with more than one growing crown. In a rosette type the result of suckers not being removed.

Mutant A plant produced either by natural or chemical means that has a different appearance to that of its parent. A sport.

Neck The main stem above the potting compost caused by the loss or removal of the lower leaves of an African violet.

Node The slightly swollen area of a main stem from which leaves, flower peduncles and branches arise.

Ovary The swollen base of the pistil wherein seeds develop.

Ovule An egg cell or female gamete in an ovary.

Parthenogenetic reproduction Reproduction without sexual union *ie* without male fertilization.

Pedicel The stalk of each individual flower.

Peduncle A flower stalk growing from a leaf axil from which the pedicels arise to give a cluster of flowers.

Petiole A leaf stalk arising from the leaf axil on the main stem.

pH value A scientific measurement of the concentrations of the hydrogen and hydroxyl ions. It expresses acidity, neutrality or alkalinity.

Photosynthesis A complex chemical reaction in green plants involving chlorophyll, light, water and carbon dioxide.

Pistil The female organ of a flower consisting of ovary, style and stigma.

Pollen parent The plant producing the pollen for cross fertilization.

Pollination The transfer of pollen to the stigma.

Red-backed leaf   Coloration of lower leaf surface caused by production of anthrocyanins.

Rootball   The mass of root and compost when a plant is grown in a pot.

Rosette leaf pattern   A symmetrical, circular arrangement of leaves.

Seed parent   The plant producing seed for cross fertilization.

Self-pollination   Pollen from a plant fertilizes the ovules of the same plant.

Semi-double flower   A flower having more than five lobes, or having a small crest or tuft of lobes around the stamens.

Sepals   Small, green, leaf-like parts forming the calyx.

Siblings   The resulting plants grown from the seed in a single seed pod.

Single flower   A flower with only five lobes.

Sport   A mutant variety of a hybrid.

Stamen   The male organ of a flower consisting of filament and anther.

Stigma   The tip of the pistil which receives the pollen in fertilization.

Stoma, stomata   A minute organ on the back of a leaf that controls the rate of transpiration by opening and closing.

Style   That part of the pistil that connects the ovary and the stigma.

Sucker   Off-set or side shoot developing from a leaf axil instead of a peduncle, and producing a multi-crowned plant if allowed to grow.

Tissue culture   See **Micro-propagation**.

Transpiration   Loss of water vapour and gases from the leaves of a plant via stomata.

Two-toned flower   See **Bicoloured flower**.

Variegate   Refers to the foliage of an African violet, the green leaves being patterned with white, cream, yellow, tan or pink.

Variety   1. A subdivision of a species, written as 'var.'; 2. Sometimes used in place of a hybrid.

Veins   Leaf tissue with the ability to carry foodstuffs, water and gases around a plant.

Vegetative propagation   Propagation by leaf rather than by seed.

APPENDICES

I SOCIETIES

The Saintpaulia and Houseplant
Society
Mrs F.B.F. Dunningham, MBE
[Hon. Secretary]
33 Church Road,
Newbury Park, Ilford,
Essex IG2 7ET (England)

The African Violet Society of
America, Inc
2375 North Street, Beaumont,
Texas 77702 (USA)

Saintpaulia International, Inc
Katrina Vollmer [Membership
Secretary]
3134 N. Greenbriar Lane,
Nashville, IN 47448 (USA)

Cape African Violet Society
Alex Duncan
14 Marion Avenue, Southfield,
7800 Cape Town (South Africa)

The African Violet Society of
Canada
Mrs. P.J. Scanlon [Membership
Secretary]
1573 Arbordale Avenue,
Victoria, British Columbia,
V8N 5J1 (Canada)

The African Violet Association
of Australia, Inc
Mrs G. Lind [Membership
Secretary]
53 Kibo Road, Regents Park,
New South Wales 2143
(Australia)

Japan International Saintpaulia
Society
Mrs Toshi Kawakami
B-604 Tsutsujigaoka-Haim,
2-13-3 Shibasaki Chofu-Shi,
Tokio 182 (Japan)

II SUPPLIERS

African Violets

The African Violet Centre
Station Road,
Terrington St Clement,
King's Lynn, Norfolk PE34 4PL
(England)

Rob's Mini-o-lets
PO Box 9, Naples, New York
14512 (USA)

Granger Gardens
1060 Wilbur Road, Medina,
Ohio 44256 (USA)

Lyndon Lyon Greenhouses
14 Mutchler Street, Dolgeville,
New York 13329–1358 (USA)

A-mi Violettes
75 Marier Street,
St-Felix de Valois,
Quebec JOK 2MO (Canada)

Reg and Dorothy Townend
35 Craigie Avenue, Padstow,
New South Wales 2211
(Australia)

Tinari Greenhouses
Box 190, 2325 Valley Road,
Huntington Valley,
Pennsylvania 19006 (USA)

The Violet Express
1440 – 41 Everett Road,
Eagle River, Wisconsin 54521
(USA)

Les Violettes Natalia
124 Ch. Grapes, Sawyerville,
Quebec J0B 3AO (Canada)
Also at: PO Box 206,
Beecher Falls,
Vermont 05902–0206 (USA)

III BIBLIOGRAPHY

Scientific Papers
Baillon in *Bull. Soc. Linn.*, Paris, 1893
Baker & Clarke in *Oliver, Fl. Trop. Afr.*, 1906
Burtt, B.L. in *Gardeners' Chronicle*, 1947
   in *Notes from the Royal Botanic Garden*, Edinburgh, 1958
   in ditto, 1964
Dummer, R.A. in *Ann. Bot.*, 1912
Engler, in *Bot. Jahrb.*, 1900
   in ditto, 1921
Haarer, A.E. in *Gardeners' Chronicle*, 1955
Hooker, J.D. in *Curtis Bot. Mag.*, 1895
Naylor, E.E. and Johnson, B. in *Amer. Journ. Bot.*, 1937
Reed, S.C. in *Journ. Hered.*, 1954
Wendland, H. in *Gartenflora*, 1893
Wilson, J.H. in *Botanisch Jourboek*, 1898

Books
Bartholomew, Pauline *Growing to Show* (A.V. Enterprises Press, revised 1987)
Clements, Tony *African Violets* (David & Charles 1988)
Coulson, Ruth *Growing African Violets* (Kangaroo Press 1986)
Halford, Joan *Growing African Violets in Southern Africa* (J.P. van der Walt
   & Son (Pty) Ltd 1991)
Robey, Melvin J. *African Violets, Gifts from Nature* (Cornwell Books 1988)

INDEX